算 × 命

歐洲與臺灣的占卜特展
展覽專刊

Calculating × Destiny

Divination in Europe and Taiwan

Vorhersagen × Schicksal

Wahrsagen in Europa und Taiwan

指導單位

主辦單位

合辦單位

以共通常民經驗，展開臺史博與國際接軌

張隆志
國立臺灣歷史博物館館長

國立臺灣歷史博物館（以下簡稱臺史博）是全臺灣唯一以「臺灣史」為核心的國家級博物館。自 2011 年開館並營運 10 年後，在 2021 年 11 月升格為三級機構。升格後的首要目標，便是「國際化」，要更積極走出臺灣，成為一個代表臺灣的、國際級的歷史博物館。而本次「算 × 命：歐洲與臺灣的占卜特展」，正是臺史博升格之後與國際連結的首檔國際展，也是臺史博首次與歐洲聲譽卓著的國家級博物館進行跨國交流，展覽的視角將臺灣的占卜文化提升置於世界中，與歐洲文化一同觀看與對話。

此次特展緣起於 2018 年，經由德國知名的漢學家、也是科技部第 10 屆「杜聰明獎」得主、德國埃爾朗根紐倫堡大學國際人文學院（International Consortium for Research in the Humanities at the Friedrich-Alexander University of Erlangen-Nuremberg）Prof. Dr. Michael Lackner（朗宓榭教授）的穿針引線下，臺史博與德國日耳曼國家博物館（Germanisches Nationalmuseum）共同合作以東西方（東亞與歐洲）共通的文化經驗與常民文化議題「預測與命運」為主題，雙邊各自策展，於德國、臺灣二地辦理展覽，隔年（2019）完成「展覽合作協議」簽訂，開啟了歷時 3 年的展覽籌備工作。最後日耳曼國家博物館於 2020 年 12 月推出「此命當何—歐亞的卜術、數術與神術」特展（Signs of the Future: Divination in East Asia and Europe），臺史博則於 2021 年 12 月接棒推出本次具有臺灣特色的占卜特展，運用豐厚的常民文物館藏及借展，增添更多臺灣在地性的史料及文物，包含臺灣原住民占卜用具、臺南府城算命巷百年老店啟明堂擇日館、日本時代將日本熊崎氏姓名學引進臺灣的白惠文等重要文物，深化臺灣占卜發展的在地面貌。

而這次合作展覽的德國日耳曼國家博物館，成立於 1852 年，專責研究與展示歐洲德語系區域的藝術、歷史、文化，是德語系最大的文化史博物館與研究中心，蒐藏有 130 萬件藏品，也是德國重要的國家博物館之一，因此此次合作對臺史博而言，是個難得的合

作機會，尤其在 2020 年起全球開始面對疫情的挑戰下，臺、德雙方如何突破跨國文物運送的艱難考驗，共同攜手，順利完成德國、臺灣二地的展覽，更是一次難能可貴的經驗，也建立起新疫情時代下國際交流合作的新模式。未來，臺史博將更致力拓展國際學術交流與國際性的館際合作，進而提升臺灣的國際知名度，讓國際及國人看見「世界中的臺灣」，也讓世界看見臺灣。

籌備過程中特別感謝德國日耳曼國家博物館 Prof. Dr. Georg Ulrich Großmann、Prof. Dr. Daniel Hess 二位前後任館長的全力支持，慷慨提供該館精彩的藏品，以及 Dr. Thomas Eser、Dr. Heike Zech、Marie-Therese Feist、Dr. Anne-Cathrin Schreck、Dr. Barbara Rök、Anja Löchner 等日耳曼國家博物館夥伴的熱情協助與支援，展覽才得以順利開展。同時也感謝明斯特大學（University of Münster）Prof. Dr. Ulrike Ludwig，提供歐洲占卜文化史的研究基礎，埃爾朗根大學的蔡芷芳小姐、張詠詠小姐、中央研究院歷史語言研究所的林玉雲編審等人於籌備期間的種種協助，中央研究院歷史語言研究所祝平一研究員在展示內容上給予許多指導，在此致上最誠摯的感謝！！

Folk History as a Bridge between the NMTH and the International Community

Prof. Dr. Lung-chih Chang

Director of the National Museum of Taiwan History

The National Museum of Taiwan History (NMTH) is the only museum in Taiwan focused on the nation's history. A decade after its official opening in 2011, the NMTH was upgraded to a level 3 institution in November 2021 with a new primary goal of internationalizing the museum in order to share Taiwanese history with the global community. *Calculating × Destiny: Divination in Europe and Taiwan* is the first international exhibition following this upgrade and represents the first collaboration between the NMTH and a world-leading European institution. In *Calculating × Destiny*, divination in Taiwan is viewed in the context of the wider world to create a conversation with European culture in particular.

The exhibition was initiated in 2018 by Prof. Dr. Michael Lackner, a renowned sinologist and winner of the Taiwanese Ministry of Science and Technology's Tsungming Tu Award in 2017. From the International Consortium for Research in the Humanities at the Friedrich-Alexander University of Erlangen-Nuremberg, it was Prof. Lackner's relentless efforts that served to bridge the NMTH and the Germanisches Nationalmuseum in Nuremberg in a collaboration around the concept of "fortunetelling" in the folk histories of the East (East Asia) and the West (Europe) with the institutes curating exhibitions in Germany and Taiwan, respectively.

An agreement was signed in 2019, marking the start of preparations that would last three years. In December 2020, the Germanisches Nationalmuseum inaugurated its *Signs of the Future: Divination in East Asia and Europe*. The NMTH opened its own exhibition of divination culture with a touch of Taiwanese element in December 2021, integrating a variety of loaned objects into its rich folk cultural collections. To provide an in-depth perspective, historical literatures and objects have been added and highlighted, including indigenous divination tools, items from the centuries-old Qimingtang in Tainan's "Fortunetelling

Alley", and objects belonging to Hui-wen Bai, a diviner who introduced Kumasaki onomancy to Taiwan during the Japanese era.

At the other end of this collaboration, the Germanisches Nationalmuseum was established in 1852, specializing in the research and exhibition of the arts, history, and culture of the German-speaking regions in Europe. It is the largest museum and research center of germanophone cultures and one of the most nationally important museums in Germany with 1.3 million items in its collection. This collaboration presented a rare opportunity for the NMTH, particularly in the face of the global pandemic and overcoming the challenge of international transportation between Taiwan and Germany that the pandemic presented. Completing the exhibitions has been an invaluable experience for both parties striving for transnational collaboration in these difficult times. The NMTH will continue to broaden its international exchange of academic research through institutional collaborations in order to enhance Taiwan's global visibility, thus underscoring Taiwan in the history of the world, while allowing the world to see Taiwan.

We would like to express our most sincere gratitude to the two directors of the Germanisches Nationalmuseum, Prof. Dr. Georg Ulrich Großmann and Prof. Dr. Daniel Hess, for their unwavering support and generosity in providing access to their extraordinary collections. We also extend special thanks to Dr. Thomas Eser, Dr. Heike Zech, Marie-Therese Feist, Dr. Anne-Cathrin Schreck, Dr. Barbara Rök, and Anja Löchner; it was their enthusiastic assistance and engagement that allowed the smooth launch of the exhibitions. Our thanks also goes to Prof. Dr. Ulrike Ludwig of the University of Münster for her comprehensive research in the cultural history of divination in Europe; Chi-fang Tsai and Yung-yung Chang at the University of Erlangen-Nuremberg; Yu-yun Lin of the Institute of History and Philology, Academia Sinica, for their outstanding support in organizing the exhibition; and Ping-yi Chu, research fellow at the Institute of History and Philology, Academia Sinica, for his extensive advice about the content for *Calculating × Destiny*.

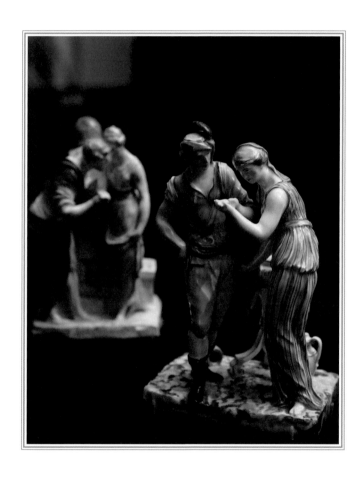

來自日耳曼國家博物館的訊息

丹尼爾・赫斯

德國紐倫堡日耳曼國家博物館館長

2020 年 12 月，我們在國立臺灣歷史博物館的慷慨出借及支援下，於德國紐倫堡的日耳曼國家博物館揭開了《此命當何──歐亞的卜術、數術與神術》（Signs of the Future：Divination in East Asia and Europe）聯展的序幕。可惜的是，在 Covid-19 的疫情對國際交通影響下，國立臺灣歷史博物館無法派人一起參加這場盛會。我們也沒料想到，就在一年後，國立臺灣歷史博物館也得在同樣的全球性陰霾下，啟動另一個雙生特展：《算 x 命：歐洲與臺灣的占卜》。這類展覽總是得提前好幾年進行規劃；而當我們開始一起策劃時，沒人想到竟然會出現全球性的疫情，直到它在 2020 年成了令人不寒而慄的現實──先是紐倫堡，然後是臺南。誰會想到預知未來這件事，竟成了這個展覽最切題的主旨？

第一位提出這個展覽的想法、並且提議和我們一起合作進行研究與展示計畫的人，是德國埃爾朗根－紐倫堡大學漢學系的朗宓榭教授（Prof. Dr. Michael Lackner）。後來，在與明斯特大學的烏爾里克・路德維希（Prof. Dr. Ulrike Ludwig）──一位早期與現代史教授──的討論下，展覽的內容也逐漸擴展到東亞與歐洲等地。而湯瑪斯・埃瑟博士（Dr. Thomas Eser），這位直到 2019 年前都是日耳曼國家博物館的科學器材負責人，更進一步為這次的合作關係帶來更多熱情與思想上的碰撞；他也為我們的展覽構思了初步的說明文字。在德國研究基金會（German Research Foundation）的資助下，他與路德維希教授一起執行了名為「傳統、觀點、與用途：17 至 21 世紀歐洲的通靈文物與意涵」（Tradition, Perspective, and Uses: Attribution of Meaning to Artefacts of Clairvoyance in Europe from the Seventeenth to the Twentieth Century）的計畫。瑪麗特蕾絲・費斯特（Marie-Therese Feist）與海克・澤赫博士（Dr. Heike Zech）則以展覽策展人的身份，為這個計畫帶來具體的成果，而瑪麗特蕾絲・費斯特更和朗宓榭教授、路德維希教授共同編輯了雙語的展覽專書。除此之外，與國立臺灣歷史博物館同仁的持續交流不僅為展覽在設計與內容上帶來寶貴的建議，也成了本次國立臺灣歷史博物館展覽的重要起點。

雖然對未來的想望是本次展覽的關注重心，我還是希望能談談本次合作早期的一些過程。我記得我們 2018 年在紐倫堡辦第一場聯合工作坊時，臺史博的張淑卿、莊佩樺與石文誠以及中研院的陳正國和林玉雲一起來訪。在紐倫堡的面對面會談讓我們有機會可以參考彼此的筆記、比較彼此的文化，並從中找到許多共通點。在占卜的研究以及如何對觀眾展示的面向上，我們彼此對於博物館在其中所扮演的角色和兩方團隊的企圖上皆有志一同，而這次在臺灣的展覽則是我們合作的最後一個里程碑。

我很高興能讓另一個國家的觀眾看到我們的展品，也很感謝這次的合作能讓我們發現這麼多彼此共享的文化遺產。儘管各自使用的方法有別，但我們對於未來抱持的疑惑是相同的。我們都對於自己、以及最親近的人的命運，感到好奇——愛情、財富、與旅行只是諸多問題其中一部分而已。從我們開始就各自的展覽進行合作以來，我們便因為 Covid-19 疫情的流行與其帶來的各種變化找到一個很明確的焦點：我們能保持健康嗎？疫情是否終將會結束？這些重大問題現在依舊說不得準，因為病毒和人一樣無法預測。隨著展覽工作而來的，還有一個非常實際的問題：押運人員可以跨國移動嗎？而答案是：不，他們不該這麼做。那麼，文物可以跨國移動嗎？好險，答案是可以。兩方團隊間專業且有效率的合作使我們重要的典藏品得以安全地展示在國立臺灣歷史博物館，我也非常感激所有參與此展的雙方工作人員。

說到本次展覽所匯集的展品，我相信參觀臺史博的觀眾會忍不住在欣賞我們的珍寶藏品時回想起自己的經歷。理解寺廟神諭（求籤）及其對東亞民眾的意義，深刻地打動了我，也影響我對歐洲占卜儀式的想法。紐倫堡的展覽讓我們的觀眾，無論是在網路上還是現場，得以了解那些對於我們的地區文化認同至關重要、卻少被討論的話題。因此，我對於阿爾布雷希特·杜勒（Albrecht Dürer）的那些知名版畫能夠被納入這個展覽感到特別開心。有人說，杜勒是透過占星術決定放棄家族的金匠事業，並成為一名畫家——而這決定絕非是對未來最安全的賭注。我相信他的《命運女神》（他的主要作品之一）揭露了他的一生是如何對占卜深信不疑。更重要的是，這個作品也深刻地體現了 16 世紀早期——一個歐洲經常發生深刻且劇烈變化的時期——對命運的普遍態度；而占星術，很顯然地，直到現今仍在東亞和歐洲有相當的能見度。在比較兩地占卜物件的方法和意義時，我對於部分展品間所顯現的驚人相似性感到驚異，例如國立臺灣歷史博物館所藏的八卦指掌雕版和約翰內斯·阿布·英達金（Johannes ab Indagine）在 1523 年的斯特拉斯堡所繪製出版、現保存於日耳曼國家博物館圖書館的掌紋圖。

我們的展覽相輔相成；它們讓我們在這個受到社交距離與各種限制的非常時期裡，為東亞和歐洲找到相知相惜之處。透過思考與討論我們共享的全球性文化遺產，這些展覽為未來的文化對話搭建了橋樑。文化跨越國界，將人們團結起來；它建造了我們之間的橋樑，使我們能夠共同塑造未來。

Message from the Germanisches Nationalmuseum

Prof. Dr. Daniel Hess

Director General of the Germanisches Nationalmuseum, Nuremberg, Germany

In December 2020, thanks to the most generous support and loans from the National Museum of Taiwan History, we opened our joint exhibition "Signs of the Future. Divination in East Asia and Europe" at the Germanisches Nationalmuseum in Nuremberg, Germany. Unfortunately, the ongoing Covid-19 pandemic made travel impossible so representatives from the National Museum of Taiwan History could not come to Nuremberg. Little did we expect that - a year on – the National Museum of Taiwan History would have to open its twin exhibition "Calculating × Destiny: Divination in Europe and Taiwan" under the same global shadow. Exhibitions, such as this, are planned years in advance. When we first started working on it jointly, a global pandemic seemed a rather unlikely scenario. In 2020, it became an unexpected but daunting reality, first in Nuremberg, then also in Tainan. Who would have known that divination might be such a topical subject for an exhibition?

It was sinologist Prof. Dr. Michael Lackner of the University of Erlangen-Nuremberg who first came up with the idea and original proposal to conduct research and organize an exhibition project in collaboration with our institution. Eventually, and thanks to conversations with Dr. Ulrike Ludwig, professor of early and modern history at the University of Münster, the topic gradually expanded to include East Asia and Europe. Dr. Thomas Eser, until 2019 the Germanisches Nationalmuseum's keeper of scientific instruments, brought additional enthusiasm and passion for debate to this partnership; he also developed the first narrative of the exhibition. Together with Prof. Ludwig, he headed a project funded by the German Research Foundation entitled "Tradition, Perspective, and Uses: Attribution of Meaning to Artefacts of Clairvoyance in Europe from the Seventeenth to the Twentieth Century". Marie-Therese Feist and Dr. Heike Zech brought the project to fruition as exhibition curators with a bilingual exhibition book co-edited by Prof. Lackner, Prof. Ludwig and Marie-Therese Feist. The continued exchange with colleagues at the National Museum of Taiwan History impacted the design and content of the exhibition markedly, and became a valuable starting point for the exhibition at the National Museum of Taiwan History.

Even though the care for the future is the key concern of the exhibition, I would also like to reflect on the early stages of our collaboration. I still remember the first joint workshop in Nuremberg in 2018, when Shu-ching Chang, Pei-hua Chuang and Wen-cheng Shih of the National Museum of Taiwan History visited us together with Prof. Jeng-guo Chen and Yu-yun Lin, Academia Sinica. The opportunity to meet in person in Nuremberg allowed us to compare notes and cultures, and find a lot of common ground. Our views on the roles of museums and the ambition of our teams concerning research on divination and its presentation to our audiences very much align. The exhibition in Taiwan is the final milestone of our collaboration.

I am delighted to make our collections accessible to an international audience, and grateful that our co-operation has brought to light so much shared cultural heritage. The methods may differ; however, our questions about the future are the same. We all wonder about our own fate and that of our nearest and dearest, especially in regards to romance, wealth, and travel. Since we started working jointly on the two respective exhibitions, we have had a clear focus, prompted by the emergence of the Covid-19 pandemic in its ever-changing permutations: Will we be healthy? Will the pandemic finally run its course? These major questions remain surprisingly unpredictable, exactly because human beings behave in unexpected ways, as does the virus. Working on the exhibition brought with it also very practical questions: Can couriers travel? It turned out: they should not. Can objects travel? Thankfully, they could. The professional and effective collaboration of our teams has meant that highlights from our collection are now safely on display at the National Museum of Taiwan History, and I am very grateful to everyone involved in both institutions who contributed to this endeavour.

When considering the objects brought together in this show, I am convinced that visitors to the National Museum of Taiwan History will find themselves reflecting on their own experiences as they encounter treasures from our collections. Learning about the Temple Oracle and its meaning for East Asian people, has profoundly touched me and inspired me to reflect more openly about divinatory rituals in Europe. The exhibition in Nuremberg has given our audiences, online and on site, an opportunity to learn about rarely discussed topics that nonetheless are essential to the cultural identity of our regions. Therefore, I am particularly delighted that Albrecht Dürer's famous prints are part of the show. According to some, Dürer trusted the stars when he decided not to be a goldsmith, which was his family's profession. Instead, he became a painter, by no means a safe bet. I believe his print of *Nemesis* – one of his major works – shows the trust he had in divination his whole life. What is more, it also poignantly sums up prevalent attitudes towards fate during the early sixteenth century, a period of profound and often violent change in Europe. Astrology, of course, remains publicly visible in East Asia and Europe to the present day. In comparing methods and meanings, I am fascinated by the extraordinary similarity of some exhibits, such as the Jade Hand print from the collections of the National Museum of Taiwan History and a diagram of palm lines devised by Johannes ab Indagine and published in Strasbourg in 1523, and now preserved in the library of the Germanisches Nationalmuseum.

The exhibitions complement each other. They have allowed us to find common ground during a period marked by restrictions and social distancing in both East Asia and Europe. By reflecting and discussing our shared global cultural heritage, the exhibitions build bridges for a continued cultural dialogue. Culture unites people across borders; it forges connections that allow us to shape the future together.

目次 Contents

002 序｜以共通常民經驗，展開臺史博與國際接軌｜張隆志

Folk History as a Bridge between the NMTH and the International
Community｜Lung-chih Chang

007 序｜來自日耳曼國家博物館的訊息｜丹尼爾・赫斯

Message from the Germanisches Nationalmuseum｜Daniel Hess

014 東方與西方的預知法門：徵兆、宗教與歷史｜朗宓榭

Traditional Ways of Prognostication, East and West:
Signs, Religion, and History.｜Michael Lackner

024 歐洲占卜簡史｜烏爾里克・路德維希

A Very Short History of Divination in Europe｜Ulrike Ludwig

036 「算 × 命：歐洲與臺灣的占卜特展」導讀｜祝平一

An Introduction to "Calculating × Destiny:
Divination in Europe and Taiwan"｜Ping-yi Chu

040 算命之前 算命之後：當「占卜」成為展覽｜張淑卿

Before the Fortune, After the Telling: An Exhibition of Divination｜
Shu-ching Chang

算 × 命：歐洲與臺灣的占卜特展
Calculating × Destiny: Divination in Europe and Taiwan

052　命與運 Destiny and Fortune

056　觀察與推算 Observation and Calculation

  057　自然現象 Natural Phenomena

  079　人體特徵 Physiognomy

  089　人為推算 Calculation

098　神靈的預示 Spiritual Guidance

  099　啟示與預言 Revelations and Prophecies

  115　扶乩與通靈 *Fuji* and Spirit Mediums

124　扭轉運勢 Changing One's Destiny

142　占卜的人們 Fortune-Telling and -Hearing

162　占卜與遊戲 Divinations and Games

178　誌謝 Acknowledgements

東方與西方的預知法門：徵兆、宗教與歷史

朗宓榭

德國埃爾朗根紐倫堡大學國際人文研究院院長／漢學系教授

國立臺灣歷史博物館這次以對話的方式，展出東方與西方各自如何在前現代與現代時期應對未知的未來。強調「現代」這個面向之所以重要，是因為現在——尤其是今日的臺灣——有許多占卜形式來自於過往，而這也正好說明了所謂「多重現代性」（multiple modernities）的概念如何讓不同文化型態免於被西方的現代性定義綁架[01]。在此，讓我們先考察東方與西方的一些基本預知元素。

徵兆與意義

關於德爾斐皮提亞（Pythia）神諭的最古老的說法，要歸功於與孔子（551-479）同時代的希臘哲學家赫拉克利特（Heraclitus，520-460）：「上主將神諭降於德爾斐，不言喻、不隱藏，但顯現於徵兆間（ὁ ἄναξ, οὗ τὸ μαντεῖόν ἐστι τὸ ἐν Δελφοῖς, οὔτε λέγει οὔτε κρύπτει ἀλλὰ σημαίνει）（赫拉克利特著作殘篇，第 93 篇）。

古希臘將阿波羅神視為皮提亞神諭的來源。他雖然對皮提亞「說」了一些什麼，但那並非是個清楚明確的「陳述」，而是一些徵兆。這些徵兆需要被解釋。如果我們能夠對其進行解讀，一切真相終將被揭示。

赫拉克利特留下的話語基本上描述了所有文化中前現代預言的本質：徵兆被傳給那些必須對其進行詮釋以預知未來的人。從這些徵兆中，我們可以推導出某種說法——但那是我們——人類——的說法，因為神諭既沒有「說」什麼，也沒有「隱藏」任何事情。

德爾斐的神諭早在赫拉克利特之前就已經存在，荷馬也早就提及該地的阿波羅崇拜，而考古結果更發現了一個自公元前 8 世紀以來就十分繁榮的遺址。中國的《易經》也有好幾個版本，其歷時甚至可能更久，也早在孔子的時代之前就已存在了。時至今日，這本帶有神諭卦象（64 卦）的《易經》仍是中國許多預知方法的核心。許多傳統文獻皆提及

---

[01] 什穆埃爾·諾厄·艾森施塔特（Shmuel Noah Eisenstadt）是第一位提出此概念的學者，其最後一篇學術文章〈多重現代性〉（Multiple Modernities）發表於：*Daedalus*（2000 年冬季號），129（1），頁 1-29。

所謂的「筮無定法」──任何徵兆都必須要與某個問題或某件事一起理解；儘管《易經》中每一個卦的建制與定義皆有一套高度複雜的規則，但正確的詮釋仍得從整體語義的脈絡（徵兆的語義脈絡！）中篩選。

「徵兆」不等同於「起因」，這是我們必須注意的區別。為了將某件事物當作一種徵兆，它必須首先從宇宙的各種「偶然性」中被移除、必須被偶然性解放，正如它本應如此。徵兆是在特定的時間點、向特定的個人或人群發出的訊息。因此，為了將某件事物理解成某種訊息，必須建立它們之間的關聯，而我們必須渴望它們帶有意義，如此，我們才能賦予徵兆意義。

占卜與宗教

司馬富（Richard Smith），最知名的東亞占卜史專家之一，曾說：「中國的所有占卜形式都與靈性有關，但有些形式更強調靈性」[02]。由此，我們也應探討占卜與宗教活動之間程度不一的關聯性。

占卜本身，就像魔法一樣，在最初並不具有任何道德意義：無論是英雄或反派都有權學習這些技術。儘管有人會強調占卜師本身的責任，但大多時候，占卜是被用來判定事情的真偽，而惡人遭遇不幸的命運則是一種道德判斷，並非必須是預知的一部分。雖然占

星術也可能帶有「宗教性」的含義（例如星宿，或認為星辰的移動與天使有關），但兩者間並沒有十分確切的關聯。因此，我們面對的是一種漸進的、非常不同的宗教性關係，而這種關係在基督教誕生後的西方文化中，似乎遠不如在美索不達米亞、歐洲古代、東亞和印度文化中那麼明顯。甲骨文上的裂痕，如果少了祭祀活動這種宗教特徵以及對「無上」權威的祈願，自然也毫無意義。而在使用《易經》占卜前，我們也得遵守那些淨化儀式，將蓍草散放在桌上，再展開神通。

儘管在風水方面，墓地的地形會影響後代的觀念，帶有某種宗教框架，但華人世界裡各種其他占卜形式與宗教信仰之間並沒有確切的關係。正如西方占星術幾乎看不到任何宗教特徵一樣，面相、易經占卜或生辰八字除了有其根深蒂固的「宇宙觀」之外，並沒有與宗教的直接關聯。在本次展出的手相圖上，我們也看不到任何對宗教性權威的依賴。

然而，求籤這件事，卻與宗教的觀念密切相關，相關的紀錄不僅可追溯至 12 世紀，就連在今日的臺灣也相當常見。與日耳曼國家博物館的展覽專書相比，在臺灣，我們幾乎不用對這樣子的習俗進行什麼冗長的解釋。但簡單說來，就是問事者要從一個裝有 64 到 100 根籤枝的籤筒中，隨機選擇其中之一，然後通過投擲「筊杯」來確認其正確性，再前往籤詩櫃（架）尋找與其序號相對應的解說。

---

[02] 司馬富（Richard Smith）（1991），《算命師與哲學家：中國傳統社會裡的占卜》（*Fortune-Tellers and Philosophers: Divination in Traditional Chinese Society*），Boulder/Colorado，頁 221。

首先，向神明問事得在寺廟裡。這個寺廟供奉的可能是一個或是多個神祇，但問題最後都會回到主祀的神祇，而不同地區常祭拜的神明也有不同。在大多時候，廟公可以幫忙解籤，但職業的算命師也常在寺廟附近擺攤。

臺灣的神祇，尤其是主責占卜的神祇，在某些方面可以與天主教會的聖人相提並論：他們或多或少都是史上有名的人，有名的原因可能是他們的美德或模範生活，為上司鞠躬盡瘁，並隨後被神化；他們常是暴死的（如媽祖或關帝），但與其他變成陰靈或惡靈的人不同，他們能在死亡的那一刻將他們的生命能量（氣）以正向的方式轉化。

占卜的社會政治地位當然可以看作是占卜和宗教關係的一種嚴峻考驗：當它們以被曲解的「現代性」名義受到遏制時，它們便處於灰色地帶，並主要透過「科學」或「文化遺產」等名義合理化自身的存在；而在臺灣、香港以及東南亞和海外的華人社群，這樣的關係可以在寺廟或其他特定專業場所（街邊攤販、工作室）等宗教環境中觀察到。在臺灣，特定廟宇甚至會在農曆新年時透過求籤詢問「國運」。

占卜與歷史

然而，寺廟中的神諭不僅只是宗教發展的見證者而已——歷史也在占卜的結果中發揮著重要作用。無疑《三國演義》之所以在廟內占卜中佔有重要地位，是因為這部小說涉及到許多關於行動的指示和決策用的工具。一份對籤文的分析便顯示，有 16% 的內容與三國的情節有關[03]。這個代表的是歷史事件的原型化：所有與這些歷史事件「主題」相符的狀況都一體適用，而每個與歷史時刻有關的神諭文本更是一種「比青銅更持久」的紀念碑（即賀拉斯（Horace）所說的「aere perennius」）。例如，「三顧茅廬」或「一箭雙鵰」這樣的表達方式就是這類特定情境的說法原型。早在你出生之前，已經有許多人尋求決策上的幫助；早在你開口請求之前，也已經出現過許多和你類似的情況。這在某種程度上也許算是令人寬心，因為你不是唯一一個面臨那些難題的人，但你也絕對不是獨一無二的存在。在這一點上，西方世界的諺語或短語對歷史事件的使用則有相當大的不同。如果要讓西方人在這種的歷史連結上與臺灣人比肩的話，大概只有讓「卡諾莎城堡」（譯注：西方諺語「go to Canossa」意指被迫屈從的狀況）或「盧比孔河」（譯注：西方諺語「crossing the Rubicon」意指「破釜沈舟」）這類畫面出現在塔羅牌上了。

然而，西方文明也有一些類似的歷史圖像，被賦予類似的象徵性力量——只是它們大多來自宗教、神話和傳說故事：我們可以發現

---

[03] 徐艷（Yan Xu-Lackner）（2020），〈三國羅曼史：歷史典故與神諭〉（Romance of the Three Kingdoms: Historical Allusions and Oracles），發表於：Michael Lackner、Kwok-kan Tam、Monika Gaenssbauer、Terry Siu-han Yip 主編，*Fate and Prognostication in the Chinese Literary Imagination*。Leiden：Brill，頁 162-177。

它們引用像是特洛伊木馬的神話（例如「小心希臘人帶的禮物」），或是「從錫拉岩礁掉進卡力布狄斯大漩渦」、「薛西弗斯的工作」（或海克力士的任務）、尼伯龍根的忠心，珀西瓦爾的同情問題、猶大之吻等典故，而在大多時候（也許不是全部），我們也往往能將寺廟神諭（求籤）的歷史典故中的「情境」與這些圖像所描述的情況進行聯想。這就是為什麼我們可能可以得出一個相反的結論──雖然現在這麼說有點言之過早──即東亞的神話故事常被轉化成歷史。這也是為什麼，自人類誕生以來，神話始終是透過歷史的角度被解讀，而我們所理解的神話充其量也只是一種次要角色而已。出現在《書經》中的大禹，可能正如許多人所認為的那樣，最初是某種爬行動物，只是後來轉變成了文化傳統中的帝皇。神話歷史化所要付出的代價便是走向神話象徵主義，而歷史變得圖式化（schematization）。

史學家黃俊傑在其〈中國歷史思維的性格特徵〉（The defining character of Chinese historical thinking）一文中，曾寫道：「中國人的思維以歷史為核心發展。在中國，人文就等同於歷史。中國人相信，我們之所以能成為人，是因為我們以一種歷史的方式去思考與行動。」[04] 這個說法看起來仍顯得相當抽象，但正是出於這個原因，我們試圖透過寺廟神諭（求籤）的歷史典故去展示這段文字非比尋常的感召力。

如果 60、64 或 100 個經典圖樣可以反映我們所面臨的情況，我們的決策方式是否也僅限於這個數量？難道不能有上千種這類計算方式？既然任何事都會發生，為什麼不乾脆完全放棄這些模式？這些問題很難有個答案；在西方文明似乎決定在占卜中放棄大部分歷史、並任由即時新聞的演算法（有時是為了商業利益，有時則是為了對抗犯罪或氣候變遷）接管未來時，東亞居民對歷史模式的頑強依戀在西方人看來也許有些「過時」。然而，以一個旨在將東亞人從解放的缺陷中釋放出來的姿態，西方人真的想要給他們提供一個揚棄歷史拓撲的後聖典──一個只考慮當下的無限演算法則聖典，或者是一個完全偶然的體系，來取代他們原有的、至少能給人方向和定位的傳統占卜方案嗎？

這個展覽呈現了臺灣傳統文化的勃勃生機以及與歐洲相應文化的驚人相似之處，而後者在很大程度上已經失去活力。自從德爾斐的神諭不再靈驗後，西方世界就此再也看不見占卜與宗教間的密切連結。然而，不管一個人的信仰為何、是否相信預知未來的古老法門，人類對於理解命運的這份渴望，總是值得深入探討的。希望本展的觀眾也都能感受到這次策展背後的研究熱情。

---

[04] 黃俊傑（2007），〈中國歷史思維的性格特徵〉（The Defining Character of Chinese Historical Thinking），*History and Theory*，46（2），頁 184。

Traditional Ways of Prognostication, East and West: Signs, Religion, and History.

Prof. Dr. Michael Lacker

Director of the International Consortium for Research in the Humanities at the Friedrich-Alexander University of Erlangen-Nuremberg

The exhibition at the National Museum of Taiwan History presents, in the format of a dialog, premodern and modern forms of coping with the future in East and West. It is important to emphasize the "modern" aspects, because numerous divinatory techniques of the past have survived, particularly in present-day Taiwan, which constitutes an excellent example for the notion of "multiple modernities" that allows for a multiplicity of cultural programs that cannot be reduced to a solely western understanding of what is modern[01]. Let us first examine some of the essential elements of prognostics in East and West.

Signs and Signification

The oldest statement that we have about the oracle of Pythia in Delphi is attributed to the Greek philosopher Heraclitus (520-460), a contemporary of Confucius (551-479): "The Lord whose oracle is at Delphi, does not say, does not hide, but gives signs" (ὁ ἄναξ, οὗ τὸ μαντεῖόν ἐστι τὸ ἐν Δελφοῖς, οὔτε λέγει οὔτε κρύπτει ἀλλὰ σημαίνει, (fragment 93).

Ancient Greece saw the god Apollo as the source of inspiration for the oracles of the Pythia. Of course he "says" something through Pythia, but this is not an unambiguous "statement", it rather takes the form of signs. These signs need to be interpreted. If we are able to interpret, nothing will be hidden any longer.

---

[01] Shmuel Noah Eisenstadt was the first scholar to formulate this concept, see his most recent article "Multiple Modernities", in: *Daedalus*, Vol. 129, No. 1, (Winter 2000), pp. 1-29

Heraclitus' sentence basically describes the essence of premodern prognostics in all cultures: signs are passed on to people who have to interpret them in order to be able to see into the future. From these signs we can formulate a statement - but that is our – human – statement, because the oracle has neither "said" anything, nor "hidden" anything.

The oracle at Delphi existed long before Heraclitus, Homer already speaks of a cult of Apollo there, and archaeological finds show a flourishing site since the 8th century BCE. The Chinese "*Changes*", which existed in several versions, are probably a little older; they, too, existed long before Confucius. The "Book of Changes" (Yijing 易經) constitutes the core of many Chinese forms of forecasting to this day. This book contains hexagrams (64 in number) accompanied by oracles. And numerous traditional sources state that "the yarrow stalks (and thus their interpretation) do not follow any fixed rule" (shi wu ding fa 筮無定法) - the sign is always to be understood in connection with a question, a certain matter; in fact, the creation of a hexagram in the "Book of Changes" follows a highly complex set of rules, but the correct interpretation is a selection from an overall semantic context (that of the signs!).

"Signs" are not "causes". That is an important difference to be noted. In order to understand something as a sign, it must first be removed from the vast universe of chance, it has to be freed from chance, as it were. A sign is a message that is given to a specific person or group of people at a specific point in time. Therefore, in order to understand something as a message, a connection has to be made, we have to desire that meaning exists and subsequently, we attribute a signification to the sign.

Divination and Religion

Richard Smith, one of the most eminent experts in the history of fortune-telling in East Asia states: "All forms of Chinese divination were spiritual, but some were more spiritual than others" [02]. It is worthwhile to deal with the more or less close affinity of divination with religious practices.

Divination per se - like magic - is initially morally neutral: its techniques are just as open to the villain as to the brave; even if there was an emphasis on the responsibility of the fortune-teller, it applied more to the exclusion of fraud, and the fact that the wicked runs into misfortune is more a moral

[02] Richard Smith, Fortune-Tellers and Philosophers. Divination in Traditional Chinese Society, Boulder/Colorado 1991, p. 221.

presumption than that it is necessarily inscribed in the prediction. Astrology can also have "religious" connotations (for example in the sense of star deities or angels moving the stars), but no compelling connection can be made out. We are therefore dealing with a gradual, and very different religious affinity, which seems to be much less pronounced in Western cultures since the beginning of Christianity than in Mesopotamia, European antiquity, East Asia and India. The oracle bone inscriptions are of course inconceivable without the explicitly religious character of the accompanying sacrifice and the invocation of "transcendent" authorities. The consultation of the *Book of Changes* could be preceded by rituals of purification, preparation of the table on which the yarrow stalks were distributed, and invocations.

It may still apply to *fengshui* that at least the idea of an influence of the topography of the tomb on the descendants has a religious affinity, but no direct reference to religion can be established for numerous other fortune-telling techniques of the culture of the Chinese-speaking world. Just as western astrology for the most part has a neutral character, physiognomics, the oracle drawn from the *Book of Changes*, or horoscopy (in the form of 八字), apart from being rooted in a general "cosmological" view of the world, have no direct proximity to religion.

For the charts on palm-reading, which are part of this exhibition, there is no imminent need for a spiritual authority either.

The temple oracle (qiuqian 求籤 or chouqian 抽籤, "request the oracle sticks" or "pull the oracle sticks") is, however, very closely connected with religious ideas and practices and has been documented since the 12th century. Needless to mention that it is widespread in present-day Taiwan. In contrast to the catalog of the exhibit at the Germanic National Museum, a lengthy explanation of this practice is dispensable in a Taiwanese context. Suffice it to say that the querist is facing a receptacle (籤筒) containing 64 to 100 oracle sticks, randomly chooses one of them, tests its reliability by throwing "moon blocks" (筊杯) and subsequently proceeds to a shrine that contains the respective serially numbered answers.

First of all, the questioning of the oracle takes place in a temple. This temple may be dedicated to one or more deities, but the questions are always directed to a deity who is "responsible" in some way, and regional preferences do also play a role. In many cases monks are available as interpreters, but professional fortune-tellers also like to settle near temples.

Taiwanese deities, especially those responsible for divination, can be compared in some respects with the saints of the

Catholic Church: mostly they are historically more or less documented persons who, due to their virtuous and exemplary way of life, act as advocates at higher authorities and were subsequently deified; in many cases (such as Mazu or Guandi) they died a violent death, but had the ability, unlike others who become uncomfortable and even vicious demons, to positively transform their life energy (qi 氣) at the moment of their death.

The social and political status of divinatory practices can certainly be seen as a kind of acid test in terms of their affinity to religion: when they are suppressed in the name of an ill-understood "modernity", they are located in a gray area and legitimize themselves primarily through recourse to "science" or "cultural heritage"; while in Taiwan, Hong Kong as well as in Chinese communities in Southeast Asia and overseas - depending on their specificity – they can be observed either in the religious environment of temples or in facilities run by experts (street stalls, studios). In Taiwan there are even temples where an oracle is asked about the "fate of the country" (guoyun 國運) for the Chinese New Year.

Divination and History

However, the temple oracle bears not only witness to religion: History, too, plays an eminent role in many of its answers. It is no wonder that *The Three Kingdoms* (三國演義) occupy an important place in the temple oracle, because this novel deals with directives of action and tools of decision. For example, in one analyzed set of oracle texts, 16% of the content related to scenes from the Three Kingdoms[03]. We are witnessing the archetypalization of historical events, valid for all the situations of existence corresponding to the "motif". Each text of the oracle relating to a moment in history is also a monument "aere perennius" (more lasting than bronze, as Horace says). Take, for example, expressions like 三顧茅廬, or 一箭雙鵰which have become archetypal articulations of a precise situation. Times before you were born, there was already someone asking for help in decision-making, times before you asked, there was always a situation similar to yours. Maybe that is reassuring, because you are not the only one facing a given situation, but you are not unique either, far from it. On this point, there definitely is a considerable difference in the use of an historical event in proverbs or locutions of the western sphere: it is only if "Canossa" or the "Rubicon"

---

[03] Yan Xu-Lackner, « Romance of the Three Kingdoms: Historical Allusions and Oracles", in: Michael Lackner, Kwok-kan Tam, Monika Gaenssbauer, Terry Siu-han Yip (eds.), *Fate and Prognostication in the Chinese Literary Imagination*, (Leiden: Brill 2020), pp. 162-177.

appeared on tarot cards that westerners would then be on a par with the Taiwanese in the treatment of history.

However, Western civilizations, too, have produced a few comparable images, imbued with a similar symbolic force - however, these come from the realms of religion, mythology and legends: let us quote the myth of the Trojan horse (therefore a "gift from the Daneans"), "to fall from Charybdis to Scylla", a "Sisyphus work" (or work of Hercules), the loyalty of the Nibelungen, the question of compassion in Perceval, the kiss of Judas - to most of these images (perhaps not all of them), we can relate a situation comparable to a "situation" in the historical allusions of the temple oracle. And this is how one might dare to draw the opposite conclusion - perhaps a little premature - namely that East Asian mythology tends to be transformed into history. This is the reason why the myth has been interpreted in a historical sense since the dawn of mankind, mythology as we understand it playing a secondary role at best. The Great Yu 大禹, who among others appears in The Classic of Shujing 書經 documents, may, as many assume, originally have been some sort of reptile, but in tradition he became an emperor. The price to pay for the historicization of the myth is the orientation towards a mythological symbolism, a schematization of History.

The historian Huang Chun-chieh 黃俊傑notes in an article on "The defining character of Chinese historical thinking": "Chinese thought is history-centered and revolves around it. In China, to be human is to be historic. The Chinese believe that we are human because we think and behave in a historical way." [04] It may still seem very abstract, and it is for this reason that we have tried to show the unusual evocative force of these words by means of the historical allusions of the temple oracle.

If sixty, sixty-four, or a hundred typical images can reflect the situations we face, aren't we limited to that number in our decisions either? How about thousands of such algorithms? Why not completely abandon any model, given that anything goes? It is difficult to provide an answer; in a situation when Western civilizations seem to have decided to give up a large part of their history, and where the algorithms of immediate news have taken over, (sometimes for commercial interests, sometimes to fight against crime or for reasons of climate change), the tenacious attachment of the inhabitants of East Asia to historical patterns may seem to westerners

---

[04] Huang Chun-chieh, "The Defining Character of Chinese Historical Thinking," *History and Theory* 46, N° 2 (2007), p.184.

to be somewhat "out of date". But, in a gesture aimed at freeing them from their emancipatory deficits, do westerners really want to offer them a post-canonical renunciation of historical topoi, an infinite number of algorithms relating to the present or a generalized arbitrary system, all supposed to replace their own schemes which, at least, promise a direction and an orientation?

The present exhibition shows the vitality of tradition in Taiwan as well as some striking parallels with European counterparts, which, for the greater part, have lost their vitality. Since the decline of the Delphic oracle, there is no close connection between religion and divination in the western sphere. However, regardless of one's belief or trust in age-old practices of coping with the future, it is worth studying the human desire to know fate. It is to be hoped that the visitors of this exhibition share the organizers' enthusiasm for this study.

歐洲占卜簡史

烏爾里克‧路德維希
德國明斯特大學宗教與政治卓越學群教授

歐洲的各種文化起源——亦或者說，世界上的各種文化起源——讓占卜出現了各種不同面貌。這些占卜的形式玲瑯滿目，從占星、塔羅、咖啡占、觀察並解讀候鳥的飛行、神諭，到用獻祭過的內臟卜卦、隨閱占卜法（隨意翻開書本查閱其中的章節）、夢占、手相，就連黑貓或是低空飛過的彗星等世上萬物都被賦予了與運勢相關的徵兆。

為了簡單描繪歐洲的占卜歷史，我們得先談談歐洲文化的延續、轉變、其悠久的傳統、蛻變，以及時代的新篇章；同時，我們也必須指出，歐洲對於占卜的根本矛盾心態，在過去幾個世紀以來並沒有減少，反而越趨增多。

延續

數百年來，各種形式的占卜都在歐洲社會裡共存著。除了在猶太—基督教傳統中佔有重要地位的「預言」外，長久以來，最主要的發展便是相信蒼穹中恆星和行星的位置變化都有其寓意。占星術的起源（與天文學的出現密切相關）可以追溯到公元前二千年的美索不達米亞人、亞述人和西臺帝國時期。那時的人們相信定期出現的天體將產生特定的影響，而天空中的異象——例如彗星和流星——則被認為帶有不祥之兆。這些現象被視為預兆——一個險惡的伏筆，一個預示未來發展（但鮮少受人歡迎）的徵兆。從人類有史以來，這些「特殊跡象」就被記錄和編纂下來，正如名為《徵兆結集》（Enuma-Anu-Enlil）的天文泥板所示，在其所收錄的系列中，記載了約七千個巴比倫的天象預兆。羅馬人關於預兆的文獻、拜占庭人關於解讀雷霆的文集，以及後來在 16 和 17 世紀流傳的關於預兆的彩色插頁，背後都有一個非常相似的想法。

同樣的，人的性格會透過人體（或是人體的特徵）顯露的概念，也常見於各種古老的文化習俗中。其中一個最鮮明的例子，是所謂的「手相占卜」，其在歷史上及世界各地都有著形式極為相似的實踐。由此看來，人們似乎不僅試圖理解手上的線條，也傾向於將手的厚度和褶皺當成體內另一個潛在自我的「鏡像」。在約翰·卡斯帕·拉瓦特（Johann Caspar Lavater，1741–1801）出版了《面相學文集》（*Physiognomische Fragmente*）後，面相和手相學更得到了全新的發展。20 世紀早期的「性格學」則更進一步的詮釋傳統中對於身體與個人命運之間的關聯性，並在納粹的種族人類學中達到駭人的高峰。總的來說，特別需要強調的是，這種將醫學（以及後來的心理學）與手相和面相聯繫起來的企圖，在 19 和 20 世紀間並非罕見。當然，在意義的建構上——也就是手相和面相中採用的解釋框架（如何使其言之有理）——經歷了一些變化，有些變化更是不容小覷。不過，如何在現行的論證與詮釋傳統中看到傳承延續的元素，對我們而言也同等重要。

最後，我們應該留意的是，超越時間而留存下來的並非只有占卜的方法與形式，還有隨之而來的，關於命與運的觀念。透過命與運的圖像，我們方能看見古老傳統延續的證據。

西方占卜史中的轉變與斷裂

將時間拉長，我們不僅能看到占卜文化延續的證據，還能看到跨時代的轉變過程。這些轉變的原因來自於整個歐洲文化的鉅變，也就是劃時代的三個主要文化進程：基督教作為羅馬帝國的國教、印刷機和活字印刷術的發明、以及歐洲的啟蒙運動。

基督教的建立與禁忌，以及預言的盛行

地中海地區的古代社會以占卜文化為其特色，而這種文化不僅高度多樣化，更與宗教習俗密切相關。然而，基督教被確立為羅馬帝國的官方宗教後，不僅逐漸突顯了宗教與各種不同占卜形式之間的差異，也加深了彼此之間的裂痕。同時，更扮演了影響占卜與歐洲社會關係的關鍵角色，使占卜的爭議性地位就此新增了另一個面向。占卜成了宗教的競爭者，而占卜者與問卜者則不得不面臨從事異端活動的指控。從事異教（即基督教之前）的占卜活動，從根本上來說，等同於對基督教及其一神信仰的背叛。在這個觀點下，占卜作為前一個時代的異教遺物，更不可能在基督教世界觀中立足。

與此同時，各基督教會與其代理人對占卜的態度也從一開始就顯得相當矛盾。一方面，教會否定所謂「命定」的概念，因為這種概念與基督教的「自由意志論」相衝突。然而，從另一方面來看，這種否定卻又必須承認，至少對上帝而言，未來的存在是確定且早已註定好的。要突破這個困境，其中一個可能的途徑便是採用猶太─基督教裡的預言文化，一種唯一豁免於人們對占卜譴責的預測形式。

儘管如此，基督教早期的最大挑戰仍在於如何處理那些行之有年的占卜活動，更需要為那些「異教徒」的預言準確性找到一種說法，或者（最好是）讓這種預言徹底消失。在羅馬時代晚期，部分占卜活動被禁止的同時，另一些則被允許繼續進行，而所謂的預言則成了國家專屬的領域。隨後，

對占卜的各種禁令紛紛下達。例如，狄奧多西皇帝（the Emperor Theodosius）在385 年頒布了一項法令，禁止人們進行臟卜（haruspicy）——在獻祭活動後用內臟，尤其是肝臟，進行占卜——而違者處死。我們很難確定那些前基督教的占卜技術在官方的打壓下延續了多久，不過，儘管這些占卜活動仍不時在查禁的名單上出現，很多習俗似乎很快就消失了。部分在禁令以外的占卜形式，尤其是占星術，雖然留存到現在，但其作為預言工具的重要性已不復從前。

然而到頭來，神聖預知的概念，在某種程度上，終究還是留有餘地，讓人們可以間接地論證。即便在宗教預言的領域之外，仍然有可能在合乎基督教理的狀況下對未來進行預測。例如，除了預言性的聲明外，上帝還經常以地震和彗星的形式傳達徵兆——或者更確切地說，是預兆。從這個角度來看，占卜並不一定被視為迷信（從一種「信仰錯誤」的意義上來了解）；對未來進行準確的預測完全是有可能的，而且在上帝允許的情況下，也確實總是準確的。

儘管仍有教會以其專業知識進行占卜的例子（例如，信仰及聽從西比拉（sibyls，女先知）和宗教預言），但基督教下的歐洲對占卜的普遍態度基本上還是處於一種矛盾的狀態。畢竟，人們相信，所謂的神蹟也有可能是來自惡魔或撒旦的詭計；上帝的旨意永遠難以捉摸，唯一絕對安全的方法就是遠離占卜師，而不是尋求他們的幫助。然而，在中世紀中期到晚期間，「預言」出現了戲劇性

的發展。這一點從大量圍繞著《啟示錄》裡關於「末日」恐怖預言的文本中可以明顯看出，而這些文本也同時具有批判當代社會的特徵。除了譴責一般大眾的不道德行為，這些文本也經常攻擊教會濫用其制度及機構身份的行為，更將教會衰弱的地位解釋為末日即將到來的確切預兆。

翻譯運動、印刷機、大眾化

好幾世紀以來，預言不僅是作為占卜最重要的形式，也替其他占卜種類帶來蓬勃的發展——例如占星術和靈籤、擇日（Tagwählerei，辨識幸運和不幸的列表）和相信預兆、姓名學（姓名算命，對姓名進行解釋）、夢占、以及其他各種不同形式的占卜。這些不同的占卜類型在中世紀晚期再次受到人們的歡迎。它們經常借鑒於前基督教時代的習俗和知識庫，並透過阿拉伯地區和拜占庭（東羅馬帝國）的學者們的知識傳播，使其變得更為興盛；而地中海東部的拜占庭維持了羅馬的文化與知識遺產長達數個世紀之久。

在 14 和 15 世紀，前面提及的種種因素促成了占卜知識深厚的積累，並進一步從義大利傳播至西班牙、法國和阿爾卑斯山以北地區。從中世紀來到近代早期（大約 1500 年），印刷機的出現不僅成了傳播知識的催化劑，使得這些占卜學問能持續累積，也導致西方歷史開始出現變革。印刷機這個新媒體對占卜的影響，可以從原本只有少數人才能習得的占卜技術變得大眾化中看出。以各種語言和方言撰寫且簡單易懂的占卜文本在

此時大量出現，為業餘的讀者們提供實用的指引。這些文本在中世紀晚期原以手稿的形式留存，但印刷機卻讓這些知識得以傳播給更廣大的讀者群。

在新大眾媒體所帶來的各種可能性和大眾化的影響下，占卜在 16 和 17 世紀的歐洲經歷了前所未有的黃金時代。越來越多人從事占卜、算命的工作，而占卜的相關用品也被商品化。占卜的大眾化不僅被印刷商和出版商當成一個不錯的小型收入來源，還使得各種占卜技術成為生活常識的一部分。

與此同時，在宗教改革期間的最後一個全盛時期（許多人認為這即是末日本身）之後，「預言」終於失去了其在占卜界的領導地位。此後，占卜的主導形式變成了各種表格化的計算方式，像是占星、堪輿、籤書（提供靈籤的解釋）等。這些形式往往旨在為未來的短期發展提供一個模糊的景象，也將人們從過往對末日的關注轉移至日常生活中的特定面向和俗世間的活動。

（歷經）啟蒙與嘲諷，仍屹立不搖

最後，在現代時期開始時（約為 1800 年左右），我們可以看到占卜迎來了第三個重要的轉變過程，並如雅努斯神（Janus）般有著雙面性。啟蒙運動的來臨，是整個歐洲大陸自有史以來，首次有思想家開始質疑人類預測未來的可能性。從此，人們對算命的態度發生了根本性的轉變。在此之前，儘管大多數人都接受占卜的實用性和有效性，它仍然是一種（或多或少）被禁止的技藝。但在啟蒙運動之後，占卜開始被視為一種謬論，一種任何用「理性」思考的人都不可能會相信的騙局。

這種信念的產生與人們開始以另一種方式理解未來息息相關。至少在某些社會論述裡，未來——這裡指的是全人類的未來，而不是個人的多變生命軌跡——不再被視為是一種命中注定。與之相反，越來越多人開始接受未來有無限可能的概念及論述。而這一發展與自然科學的興起，以及從 17 世紀中葉開始逐步建立的一種理解世界的新模式密切相關。

在這樣子的背景下，尤其是在啟蒙運動對各種占卜和魔法技藝的反對下，歐洲社會產生了一種對於超驗現象的新態度。隨著這個時代多元的教育與學習方式，許多學術論文不再使用拉丁文書寫，轉而改用有更廣大市場的白話文進行印刷出版；同時，隨著教會權威的限縮，啟蒙運動也為新一波秘學（Hermetic arts）的接受和應用拓展了一些空間。我們可以藉此看出，作為啟蒙運動下的意外結果，占卜的專業知識是如何在這一時期再次擴展並變得更容易被大眾取得。

除了有悠久傳統的那些占卜形式外，這一時期還出現了一些新的方式，例如牌占（cartomancy，用撲克牌算命）。而用咖啡渣和茶葉卜卦的「杯占」（tasseomancy）也是這段期間才出現的新占卜方法。同時，雖然透過靈媒進行占卜並不是這時才出現的新發明，但在 19 世紀和到 20 世紀初卻出現了一時蔚為風潮的新算命方式：磁性夢遊（magnetic somnambulism）。在這之後，是一場與神秘主義一起出現的「真」科學運動，用以理解和研究所謂的「超自然現象」。為了想進一步瞭解靈性世界與超自然現象，他們會在嚴格的「科學」條件下舉辦公開的降神會（seance）進行觀察，留下科學記錄和監測，而所有靈媒都會使出渾身解術讓緊張兮兮的觀眾留下一些懸念。這個時代有無數科學家對神秘學有著濃厚的興趣，並在不同的論壇上進行有關靈學（spiritualism）、心靈感應（telepathy）和各種超自然現象的討論。

除了對超自然現象的信仰外，經典的預言也在 19 世紀捲土重來，伴隨著人們對世界末日一說的重新關注。最為人熟知的例子則包含摩門教、基督復臨安息日會、以及「耶和華見證人」等教派中關於世界末日即將到來的預言文本。

儘管占卜一再成為啟蒙思想家批評的目標，儘管有著各種新興的科學和解釋世界的方法，儘管「大數據」的預測模型已成了最具優勢的未來規劃工具，占卜仍舊在現代化的各種浪潮和流行中留下其印記，並持續至今。各式各樣占卜形式的交融構成了當代歐洲社會的其中一個特徵，而那些有著悠久歷史的占卜形式更吸收了來自東亞、印度和美洲的傳統文化。同時，至少自 1970 年代的新世紀運動（New Age movement）以來，流行／青少年文化中的神祕元素

（esoterica）也不斷增加。現代西方世界從此成為眾多問卜者的家園，他們為大眾提供服務，也為圖書市場貢獻了各種出版物。與神秘主義相關的聚會（esoterica fairs）參加人數創下歷史新高、具有透視能力的人開始主持自己的電視節目，而社交媒體平台、電腦軟體、應用程式，和各種短片更提供讓廣大民眾能輕鬆學習如何利用姓名、撲克牌和咖啡渣等媒介進行傳統的占卜方式。在研究這些趨勢的同時，我想我們必須承認，儘管現代社會可能很少公開鼓勵占卜，人們仍然會進行各式各樣的占卜活動──無論是當作一種消遣娛樂、一種真誠的諮詢，或是當做宗教實踐的一環。即便占卜在今日可能會招致蔑視和輕信，或有可能被當成詐財的工具，但它絕對不會消失！

A Very Short History of Divination in Europe

Prof. Dr. Ulrike Ludwig

Cluster of Excellence "Religion and Politics", University of Münster

From their diverse early origins, every culture in Europe – indeed, the world – has given rise to various forms of divination. Their forms are astonishingly numerous and diverse: astrology, tarot, reading coffee grounds, interpreting the flight of birds, consulting oracles, inspecting sacrificial entrails, stichomancy (the selection at random of passages in books), dream interpretation, chiromancy (palmistry) – as well as the belief in a whole range of good and bad omens, such as black cats and low-flying comets.

In order to sketch a very short history of divination in Europe, it is important to talk about continuities and transformation, long lines of tradition, radical disruptions, and new beginnings. However, it is also necessary to note the profound notes of ambivalence that have tended to increase rather than lessen over the centuries.

Continuities

Many types of divination having co-existed with European societies over the course of many centuries. In addition to prophecy, which formed a substantial line in the Judeo-Christian tradition, the primary ongoing thread is the longstanding belief in the underlying significance of the changing positions of stars and planets in the firmament. The beginnings of astrology (closely intertwined with the advent of astronomy) go back as far as the second millennium BCE, to the time of the Mesopotamians, Assyrians, and the Hittite Empire. Whereas heavenly bodies that reappeared regularly were believed to exert predictable influences, unusual phenomena in the sky – comets and shooting stars, for example – were thought to have an ominous character. Such phenomena were viewed as portents – a sinister foreshadowing, an omen announcing future (and seldom welcome) developments. From the dawn of human history, people took to recording and compiling these 'special signs', as we know from the collection of Enuma-Anu-Enlil, which forms a compendium of some 7000 Babylonian omens. A very similar idea lies behind Roman literature on omens, Byzantine collections on the interpretation of thunder, and later the colourfully illustrated broadsides on portents circulated in the 16th and 17th century.

Likewise, the idea of attributing signs of character to a person's body (or specific features or signatures of the body) is an ancient practice encountered across many cultures. A particularly clear example of this is chiromantic divination, a practice that has assumed distinctly similar forms throughout history and across the world. It seems that people are predisposed to understanding not only the lines but also the elevations and folds of the hand as a 'mirror' of the potential self within. *Physiognomy and chiromancy* were even given a new lease of life with the publication of the *Physiognomische Fragmente* by Johann Caspar Lavater (1741–1801). Early 20th-century characterology took the traditional understanding of the link between the body and personal fate one step further, reaching its dreadful climax in Nazi racial anthropology. Generally speaking, it should be stressed that attempts at linking medicine (and later psychology) with chiromancy and physiognomy were not uncommon in the 19th and 20th century. Of course, sense making – the interpretational

frameworks employed in chiromancy and physiognomy – underwent changes, some of them considerable. Yet it is also important to highlight the elements of continuity seen in the ongoing traditions of argumentation and interpretation.

Finally, it should also be noted that it is not only particular forms and techniques of divination that have been maintained through time, but also accompanying concepts of luck and fate. Here, right through to the iconography of luck and fate, there is evidence of continuity with ancient traditions.

Transformations and Breaks in the History of Western Divination

Over the long term, there is evidence not only of continuities but also massive transformational processes. These transformations were sustained by fundamental changes affecting the whole of European culture. It is possible to identify three principal developments that marked epochal caesuras: the establishment of Christianity as the state religion of the Roman Empire, the invention of the printing press and moveable type, and the European Enlightenment.

Establishment of Christianity, Prohibitions, and the Rise of Prophecy

Ancient societies in the Mediterranean area were characterized by a culture of divination that was both highly diverse and intimately connected to religious practices. However, the establishment of Christianity as the official religion of the Roman Empire in late antiquity led to a growing rift between religion and forms of divination. This would henceforth play a crucial role in society's relationship to divination in Europe, whose contested status had now acquired an entirely new dimension. Divination was now in competition with religion, while its practitioners and their clients now had to reckon with accusations of engaging in unchristian activities. Initially, the suspicion was that people were tinkering with pagan (i.e., pre-Christian) forms of divination, which equated to a betrayal of Christianity and its faith in one God. This view held divination to be a relic of the previous era's paganism, which had no place anymore in the Christian world.

At the same time, the attitude of the Church(es) and their representatives to divination was ambivalent from the very outset. For, on the one hand, the Church rejected the idea of fate, since it contradicted the Christian notion of free will. Yet this rejection still had to be reconciled with the certainty that, for God at least, the future already existed. One possible way out of this conundrum was through the tradition of Judeo-Christian prophesy, widely regarded as the one form of prognostication exempted from the general condemnation of divination.

Nonetheless, the major challenge of these early years was to find a way of dealing with these well-established divinatory practices, particularly the need to account for the accuracy of predictions made by 'pagans', or – even better – to prevent such predictions from ever seeing the light of day. During the late Roman period, some divinatory practices were prohibited while others were allowed to continue, and a state monopoly emerged in the realm of prediction. There then followed outright bans: for example, a decree was issued by the Emperor Theodosius in 385, forbidding, on pain of death, the practice of haruspicy: the reading of entrails, particularly livers, after sacrifice. It is difficult to know for certain just how long pre-Christian fortune-telling techniques continued to be practiced after the official clampdown. However, despite in later years being referred to intermittently in catalogues of prohibitions, it seems likely that many of these practices quickly fell by the wayside. Other forms remained in use, particularly astrology, although its importance as a tool for prophesying diminished.

Ultimately, however, the concept of divine foresight also provided a degree of leeway that allowed people to argue indirectly that, even outside the realm of religious prophecy, it was still possible and permissible to foretell the future. There was space to argue, for example, that beyond prophetic pronouncements, God was also wont to give signs – or, rather, portents – in the form of earthquakes and comets, for example. From this perspective, divination was not necessarily regarded as a superstition (in the sense of a false belief). Accurate predictions were entirely possible, and indeed always were accurate when permitted by God.

While there were instances of the Church making use of divinatory expertise (deferring to sibyls and religious prophecies, for example) the prevailing attitude to divination in Christian Europe was one of fundamental ambivalence. After all, it was agreed, a divine sign could always turn out to be the product of demonic or even satanic prompting and trickery; God's will would always remain inscrutable, and the only absolutely sure way to be safe was to keep away from fortune tellers, not seek them out. Nevertheless, there was a dramatic upsurge of prophecy during the High and Late Middle Ages. This is evident from the large number of texts generally themed around the horrors anticipated with the imminent 'end of days' as foretold in Revelations, but was also marked by an increasingly critical perspective on contemporary society. As well as targeting the immorality of the general population, the texts often attacked the abuses of the Church as an institution. Indeed, the woeful state of the Church was interpreted as a sure portent of the coming Apocalypse.

Translation Movement, Printing Press, and Popularization

For centuries prophecy was the pre-eminent form of divination, but with many other practices continuing to flourish in its wake, such as astrology and the casting of lots, *Tagwählerei* (tables identifying lucky and unlucky days) and the belief in portents, onomancy (interpretation of names), the interpretation of dreams, and many other practices. This other side of divination experienced a revival in the Late Middle Ages. Such practices often drew on customs and repositories of knowledge from the pre-Christian era, which were accelerated by the transfer of learning undertaken by scholars in the Arab world and Byzantium, which over the course of centuries had maintained Rome's cultural and intellectual legacy in the eastern Mediterranean.

In the 14th and 15th century, these various factors brought about a massive accumulation of knowledge in various forms of divination, which spread beyond Italy into Spain, France, and the region north of the Alps. As the Middle Ages gave way to the early modern period (around 1500), this period of sustained knowledge accumulation was complemented by the arrival of the printing press, the catalyst of that knowledge's dissemination and a transformative moment in Western history. The new medium's impact on divination could be seen in the enormous popularization of divination techniques that had once largely been the preserve of learned circles. This is evident most of all in the proliferation of easily understandable versions of texts, which were published in the vernacular of various languages and served to provide practical instructions for lay readers. Such texts had existed in manuscript form in the Late Middle Ages but the printing press now made it possible to reach a readership of an entirely different scale.

Due to these new mass-media possibilities and the resultant process of popularization, divination in 16th and 17th-century Europe experienced an unprecedented golden age. More and more fortune tellers plied their trade, while divinatory products were commoditized. This not only proved to be a nice little earner for printers and publishers, but also ensured that a variety of divinatory techniques became common knowledge. At the same time, prophecy finally lost its pre-eminent position in the field, following its final heyday during the Reformation (which many had come to view as the end of days

itself). Henceforth, the scene was defined primarily by practices involving tabulated computations, such as astrology, geomancy, and lot books (for the casting of lots). These tended to aim at providing a glimpse of the more immediate future, with the erstwhile preoccupation with the end of time giving way to a greater focus on specific, compartmentalized aspects of people's everyday lives and mortal interactions.

Enlightenment, Mockery – Yet No End in Sight

Finally, at the dawn of the modern era (from around 1800), it is possible to observe the onset of a third and thoroughly Janus-faced process of transformation. The Enlightenment marked the first time in European history when thinkers across the continent questioned whether it was reasonably possible for anyone to foretell the future at all. Consequently, public attitudes to fortune telling underwent a fundamental shift. Divination had previously been a (more or less) forbidden art, albeit one that was widely practised and generally accepted as valid. Following the Enlightenment, however, divination came to be viewed as a fallacy, a deception that no 'rational' thinking person could possibly hold true.

This belief was closely associated with a transformation in the way people understood the future. At least in certain areas of social discourse, the future – pertaining here to all humankind rather than the vagaries of each human life – was no longer seen as pre-determined. Increasingly accepted instead was a concept of the future as theoretically open-ended. This development was intimately linked to the rise of the natural sciences, and the incremental establishment from the mid-17th century of new models for understanding the world.

But against the backdrop of these developments, and particularly the Enlightenment-inspired push against various forms of divination and magic, there emerged a new social attitude towards transcendental phenomena. As a result of the era's increasingly pedagogical approach to learning, the continuing profusion of scholarship no longer written in Latin and instead in the vernacular, the growing market for the printed word, and efforts to limit ecclesiastical authority, the Enlightenment created spaces for the reception and application of a new wave of Hermetic arts. It is thus possible to identify how divinatory expertise once again expanded and became more accessible in this period, this time as an unintended corollary of the Enlightenment.

Alongside longstanding forms of divination, the period also saw the rise of new practices such as cartomancy (fortune telling with playing cards). Known as tassomancy, the reading of coffee grounds and tea leaves was another new form of fortune telling from this period. Divination practised by mediums was not an innovation of this period, although an entirely new facet of the form emerged with magnetic somnambulism, a striking and modish phenomenon of the 19th and early 20th century. Emerging alongside occultism was a genuine scientific movement that set out to understand and research 'supernatural phenomenon' in precisely these terms. At public seances observed under strict 'scientific' conditions, mediums of every description would show off their skills to a spooked audience aquiver with suspense. By documenting and monitoring these seances, it was hoped that more could be learned about the world of spirits and supernatural phenomena. Numeros scientists of this time – showing a lively interest in the occult, and engaging in discussions in a variety of forums about spiritualism, telepathy, and the wide panoply of paranormal phenomena.

Alongside the belief in the supernatural, the 19th century also witnessed a remarkable comeback of classical prophecy – and with it, a renewed preoccupation with the end of the world. Prominent examples of this are prophetic texts about the near end of the world by the Mormons, the Seventh-day Adventists, or even the "Jehovah's Witnesses".

Despite divination having been repeatedly targeted for criticism by Enlightenment thinkers, despite the rise of science and new ways of explaining the world, and despite how planning for the future has become dominated by predictive models based on 'big data', divination has left its mark on modernity in a series of waves and fashions. This is no less true of recent history. A characteristic feature of contemporary European society is the colourful mix of different forms of divination, in which long-established practices have been complemented by the enhanced influence of traditions from East Asia, India, and the Americas. There has also been a rise in esoterica, which has been part of pop/youth culture since at least the beginnings of the New Age movement in the 1970s. The modern Western world has since been home to numerous practitioners of divination, who offer their services to the general public and furnish the book market with all manner of publications. Esoterica fairs are attended in record numbers, clairvoyants host their own TV shows, while social media channels, apps, and videos give broad swathes of the population access to such traditional practices as name interpretation, cartomancy, and reading coffee granules. In studying these trends, one must acknowledge that, although modern society may have very few open advocates of divination, divinatory practices are nevertheless in abundance – be it as playful entertainment, a serious form of counselling, or as an element of religious practice. Divination today may attract scorn and credulity, may be exploited commercially and as a means of deception – but it certainly hasn't disappeared!

「算×命：歐洲與臺灣的占卜特展」導讀

祝平一
中央研究院歷史語言研究所研究員

命運是什麼？能預測嗎？可掌握否？前知未來，改變命運，是人類千百年來內心深切的渴求，占測未來的技術因而普遍存在於人類文化中。本特展透過各式占卜文物，顯現歐洲與東亞的人們如何思索命運，預測未來，以求在充滿不確定性的生命之海，成為掌舵者。

占卜預設了冥冥之處，有著宰制人類命運的力量。如何將自己的祈願傳遞給這股力量，甚至左右祂的動向，一直是占卜技藝的核心。直接向祖先、鬼、神祈訴自己的願望，或偵知祂們的動向，是人類最古老的占測方式。中國商代的甲骨文、希臘神廟的神諭，皆是早期人類卜筮的遺跡。

然而神靈無形，旨意難測，人們因此必須藉由自然—如天象、山川、動物、植物、人身—或人為的媒介—筊杯、塔羅牌、水晶球—以偵知神靈的意旨，由此發展出星占、風水、紫微斗數等卜術。能感通神靈的人則成為有規律或隨機兆象的詮釋者；這些詮釋積累成算命的知識，展現了不同文化的卜算技藝和

其中蘊涵的宇宙觀。

古代占測之事，皆為特定階層所壟斷。卜史身在職官，知識家傳，地位高崇，因為他們身繫國運。中國古代的人相信卜者的素質是能否準確占測的最重要因素。不過，大約在戰國時代，民間卜者越來越多，而卜官的地位卻江河日下。由於重視卜者在算命中的角色，後代的卜書常依托上古名家之秘傳，以宣傳他們的作品和技術。占卜書的另一個特色是不斷地重抄改編，並藉此發明新而略有差異的理論。由於占筮是相當普遍的文化現象，占卜技術也隨著文化交流而互相影響。

在今日的除魅世界中，人們常認為占卜不是迷信就是意志薄弱者的心靈雞湯。其實，史上批評算命者，代不乏人，但皆非因為上述的理由。在歐洲，卜人何能測度上帝的全知全能？此乃神學上之不可能，亦為教會所禁制。東亞各國也常禁止占測國運，天文曆書尤為屬禁。但是，占算個人的命運則可。此外，批評占算亦有知識上的理由。如果未來能知，是否意味命定？如果命定，那前知又

有何意義？如因前知影響了人的行為，改變未來的軌跡，那麼原先的預測豈非失算？其次，卜人果能前知，何不憑一技，追求一己之福？再者，人能若因算命而趨吉避凶，那麼仰賴占卜豈不勝於遵守倫理規範？

然而，禁止歸禁止，批評歸批評，占卜卻從不曾消失。即便今日科技文明大開，人們也不曾對算命卻步。甚至除了趨避惡運外，更希望提前得知命運的訊息，藉此改變未來。也因科技進步，許多算命規則可以電腦推算，使占卜遊走在宗教、魔術、娛樂與科學之間，深植於不同階層人們的日常生活之中。也許不可知的未來，是人們永恆的焦慮；不論多麼稀微，總希望有訊息，讓人採取行動，降低風險。算命因而不也是人類自主意志的展現？

An Introduction to "Calculating × Destiny: Divination in Europe and Taiwan"

Ping-yi Chu

Research Fellow, Institute of History and Philology, Academia Sinica, Taiwan

What is fortune? Is it predictable? Is it manipulable?

Foretelling the future—and thereby altering it—has been fundamental to human desire for thousands of years. Forms of divination exist in almost all civilizations. Using various objects of divination, this exhibition reveals how people across Europe and East Asia considered their destinies and predicted their futures, hoping to take control of their lives in the face of incredible uncertainty.

The practice of divination presupposes that a higher power dominates human destiny. Making one's desires known to that power—even nudging it in the right direction—has always been at the core of the art. Tortoise shell inscriptions from China's Shang Dynasty and the Oracle of Delphi in Greece provide us traces and evidence of the long history of divination.

Deities are invisible, their will unpredictable. People rely on all sort of mediums to detect the will of the gods, from natural phenomena, such as the weather, mountains, water, animals, vegetation, and the human body, to man-made objects, including moon blocks, tarot cards, and crystal balls. Practitioners who could perceive divine messages became interpreters of spiritual signs. Various forms of fortune-telling knowledge emerged from the practice of divination, such as astrology, *fengshui*, and *ziwei doushu*. These different types of knowledge reveal not just the art of divination, but more broadly the cosmologies of various cultures.

In many ancient societies, certain classes monopolized the practice of divination. With inherited family knowledge, diviners and historians in ancient China, for example, were esteemed officials because they were crucial to the destiny of the ruling regime. The diviner's talent, it was believed, was the key factor in accurate divination. By the Warring States period (c. 475-221 BCE), however, non-governmental fortune tellers emerged, while the authority of the traditional diviners was increasingly contested. The pivotal position of the diviner meant that books of divination were often claimed to be passed down secretly from renowned ancient figures, containing their techniques and ideas. Among these books, one common trait was the recycling of texts and the multiple reinvention of theories that diverged from previous texts. Since divination is a common phenomenon across cultures, these techniques reflect cultural exchange and transformation.

In our disenchanted contemporary world, divination is often considered superstitious or chicken soup for the weak-minded souls. Historically, however, divination received more diverse forms of criticism. In Europe, some believed that a human could never understand the omnipotent mind of God. Christian theologians thus considered divination impossible, and the Church prohibited the practice. In East Asia, while regimes allowed fortune-telling for individuals, various regimes forbade divining the future of the state, banning, for instance, the practice of publishing private calendars and almanacs.

Debates about divination have also intersected with central philosophical disputes about what humans can or cannot know. For example, if the future can be anticipated, it is destined, and if it is destined, any predictions about it are futile. Moreover, if the trajectory to the future can be altered through anticipatory action, would the prediction still be valid? If a diviner can tell someone's future, why don't diviners use the skill to make a fortune for themselves? And if all misfortune can be avoided through fortune telling, would relying on divination not be more effective than abiding by any code of ethics?

Despite the various bans and criticisms, divination has never disappeared. Even in today's era of advanced technology, it continues to be widely embraced. Through divination people hope to avert misfortune, learn instructions for life, and prepare for their future. Today, divination belongs to the stuff of everyday life, as computer programs and other technologies offer people from all walks of life predictions for their fates, morphing it into something that lies at the intersection of religion, magic, entertainment, and science.

Perhaps we will always be anxious about tomorrow. Even the skeptics among us look for signs to help us determine what actions we should take and how to reduce risks we might encounter. Looked at this way, might divination count as the revelation of free will?

算命之前 算命之後：
當「占卜」成為展覽

張淑卿

國立臺灣歷史博物館展示組助理研究員

算命之前

談到占卜、算命，是臺灣人聊天時、報章雜誌上經常討論的話題，特別在混沌不安的年代，更是一般人關心的熱門議題。以找工作的「yes123 求職網」為例，該網站近幾年持續針對求職者進行了職場命理與工作方向的網路問卷調查，最近一次調查時間為 2021 年 12 月[01]，發現臺灣 78% 上班族有算命的經驗，平均每人算命次數達 4.4 次，同時其中 76% 的人相信風水，可見占卜文化在當代臺灣的普及性與流行性，大多數人「寧可信其有，不可信其無」，都想掌握先機、預知未來運勢的走向，算命成為臺灣人很普遍、共通的生活經驗。

如此日常、輕鬆的課題，在 2018 年夏天德國漢學家朗宓榭教授（Prof. Dr. Michael Lackner）拜訪國立臺灣歷史博物館（以下簡稱臺史博）之後，變成一個被「正經」看待、跨文化研究的展覽主題，朗教授在臺灣找尋合作夥伴的過程中，拉起了德國日耳曼國家博物館（Germanisches Nationalmuseum）與臺史博合作的因緣。從那年起，二館展開了籌備的策展工作，以東西方占卜文物比較作為策展核心概念，規劃東西方占卜可以對話的子題，相互提供二館精彩的館藏文物，並針對德國、臺灣二地觀眾的屬性與文化背景，在同一主題下各自發展展示內容，希冀藉由文化比較的手法，顯現歐洲與東亞臺灣的人們如何思索命運的課題，並讓二地觀眾相互理解東西方的文化觀與世界觀。

拆解「算」與「命」

命運是什麼？

從過去到現在，對於未來動向的預測，與命運本質的探索，始終是不同文明社會感興趣的課題。有人認為「命是天生的、不能改，運可以變」，但人的命運早已決定嗎？有沒

---

[01] 楊宗斌，〈拜神！82% 覺得有助求職 七成六信風水！ 待遇差 15% ！62% 職場迷航！四年找到方向〉，職場情報站—yes123 求職網，https://www.yes123.com.tw/admin/white_paper/article.asp?id=20220106083434，2022/01/07。

有什麼方法、原理或計算公式，可以讓人們預測、改變未來呢？為了掌握命運，東、西方人們在不同的文化脈絡與社會環境下，發展出各種占卜的技術與方法，試圖解答人生的問題。

然而面對人生可能的風險，東西方人們是如何趨吉避凶？又有哪些人參與了占卜活動？參與的占卜者與問事者對於預測結果與命運是如何看待呢？占卜如此古老的文化，對於當代社會具有什麼樣的文化意涵？

上述種種問題，正是策展人對於命題的思考與提問，因此展名特意拆解「算命」二字，取名為「算 × 命：歐洲與臺灣的占卜特展」，希望呈現展覽想要談的 2 個核心概念—「算」與「命」。「算」指的是占卜各種計算／運算的方法與技術，「命」則代表命運觀、宇宙觀，即透過占卜技術的文物，看見文物背後所反應出東西方文化的發展、以及歐洲人與臺灣人的生命觀、世界觀，而不著重於占卜技術原理的探討上。

此外，由於占卜在歐洲與臺灣二地有著高度差異的發展，對臺灣觀眾而言異文化雖可以帶來新奇感，但如何讓對歐洲文化背景陌生的觀眾，易於理解，不會有文化隔閡、難以同理的情形產生，是展覽的一大挑戰。因此展示策略上採取以東西方共通經驗作為對話基礎，加強臺灣在地知識的補充，將展覽內容分為命與運、觀察與推算、神靈的預示、扭轉運勢、占卜的人們、占卜與遊戲等 6 大單元，希望透過歐洲與臺灣文物並陳比較的

手法，輔以影片、音樂、趣味性的互動裝置等不同展示素材，讓臺灣觀眾瞭解習以為常的算命文化是什麼，同時更藉由他者文化，反觀、發現在地文化的可貴之處。

東西比一比

值得一提的是東西方占卜文物的對照，是子單元主要呈現的故事。我們試圖找到可以對比、對話的文物，例如命盤、手相、神諭、辟邪物等，讓觀眾發現東西方占卜文化的共通性與差異性，當然也有同中有異之處。以下以年曆表與護身符為例，簡略說明東西方如何採取相似的預測方法，卻有不同的文化特色。

1. 年曆表

就自然現象的觀察而言，占星一直是東西方共同觀測的對象，也各自發展出一套曆算方法與天文學，同時民間都有使用年曆（農民曆）的習慣，依循曆表上的吉時吉日，作為生活行事的重要參考指南。

1951 年春牛圖曆表
大圖請另參閱本書第 68-69 頁。臺史博 藏

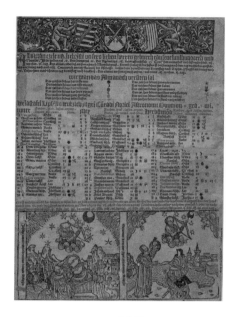

1509 年年曆
大圖請另參閱本書第 72 頁。日耳曼國家博物館 藏

1624 年或 1630 年農民曆
大圖請另參閱本書第 73 頁。日耳曼國家博物館 藏

以臺灣的「1951 年春牛圖曆表」與歐洲的「1509 年年曆」、「1624 年或 1630 年農民曆」等單張年曆表作一比較，臺灣主要標記的內容是春牛芒神圖、二十四節氣、胎神位置、及適合開市、祭祀、出行、安葬、作灶、動土、入宅、探病、嫁娶、安床、栽種…等日期；中世紀歐洲部分則標記有天主教的聖人日、月相盈虧變化、及適合放血、服藥、洗澡、斷奶、播種的時間，可說二者方法相同、觀測重點略有不同，臺灣人生活各方面都著重擇日取吉，歐洲則反應出中世紀時期人們認為身體與星象相對應的觀點，當進行放血、服藥時，需要配合占星最佳時間進行；對東西方人們而言，什麼是生活重要的事，有著不同的文化觀。

2. 護身符

為了趨吉避凶，歐洲與臺灣有些共通的做法，例如配戴、或擺設護身符。做法上，臺灣漢人社會受到道教影響，以平安符、治病符、安胎符……等符咒最為常見，歐洲則以動物、植物、寶石製作。有趣的是華人世界使用符咒治病的習俗，在歐洲也有相似的情形，18-20 世紀的歐洲人會在朝聖地購買印著聖母或聖母子肖像的護身符（Schluckbildchen），浸泡在水中溶解，並加在食物中，餵給生病的孩子或牛隻吃，或放在身上，作為民間醫療的方式之一，這也是在天主教允許下的魔法替代品。

南鯤鯓代天府
五府千歲版印平安符
臺史博 藏

三奶夫人斬煞治病符
臺史博 藏

可食用的護身符
日耳曼國家博物館 藏

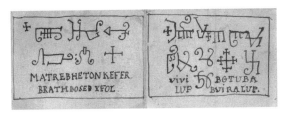

帶有符咒的護身符
日耳曼國家博物館 藏

算命之後

算命之後，大家最常問的一句話是「算的準不準？」許多人把算命結果當成重要的參考依據，但也有人鐵齒不信，究竟占卜、算命是一種迷信、陋習？還是指引人生的明燈呢？這樣的問題，在當代有了開放性的解讀。

隨著科技的發達，世界各地往來交通的便利，全球文化交流更加密切，也促使不同地區的占卜文化相互傳播、影響，占卜有了更多元的面貌。以臺灣為例，西方的塔羅牌與占星學在 1980 年代後期傳入臺灣，成為近 30 年來年輕人喜愛的占卜方式，更是社交聯誼的好話題。同時臺灣漫畫家也參與塔羅牌的繪製，例如游素蘭、德珍、林青慧等人，開始有了臺製塔羅牌的發行。而占卜文本的通俗化、趣味化，平面媒體、電視節目與網路帶動的算命風潮，皆推動臺灣占卜走向現代化、商業化、大眾化、娛樂化發展的趨勢 [02]。

此外，數位改變了人們對占卜的思考與想像，解讀不再是占卜者專有的權力，大家可以直接透過線上算命與求籤網站，快速且主動地解讀自己命運的答案，甚至將預測結果發布在臉書、IG 等社群媒體，作為凸顯個人特質、表彰自我的一種方式。在當代臺灣，占卜不再只是預測未來的方法而已，更具有療癒心靈、追尋自我生命意義、個人內在認同等更深層的文化意涵。

最後，希望大家會喜歡這個展覽，從占卜的過程中，找到自己的生命之鑰。

---

[02] 李佳穎，2015。蕭湘居士之相命活動及其相學（1976-2014），頁 62-74。臺北：臺灣師範大學歷史研究所碩士論文。

Before the Fortune, After the Telling: An Exhibition of Divination

Shu-ching Chang

Assistant Curator, Exhibition Division, National Museum of Taiwan History

Before the Fortune

Divination and fortunetelling are topics that appear on a daily basis in conversations and newspapers in Taiwan. They are brought up with extra enthusiasm in troubled times. An online survey regarding job-seekers' career directions and their use of divination at work has been conducted over the past few years by the Taiwanese job-bank website "Yes123". The latest results from December 2021 found that 78% of office workers have experience with fortunetelling, with an average of 4.4 engagements in divination per person. 76% also believe in *fengshui* [01]. This survey highlights the popularity of divination culture in Taiwan today. To get ahead of events and know what lies ahead, most people want to believe in divination, making fortunetelling one of the most commonly shared experiences among Taiwanese.

This subject matter, accessible and relatable to the public at large, became the topic of a cross-cultural exhibition after a visit to the National Museum of Taiwan History (NMTH) by German sinologist Prof. Dr. Michael Lackner in the summer of 2018. It was his search for a partner in Taiwan that led to a collaboration between the NMTH and the Germanisches Nationalmuseum. Since then, the two museums have been working together to create an exhibition comparing objects of divination in the East and the West. Subthemes for the conversation between the two cultures were planned, and relevant items from their respective collections identified. The characteristics and cultural backgrounds of audiences in both Germany and Taiwan were also considered in the exhibition's development. It is hoped that the comparative cultural approach of the exhibition will reveal how the people of Europe and Taiwan contemplate fate and guide audiences in

---

[01] Zong-bin Yang. (2022, January 7). Asking gods! 82% of people find it helpful in job hunting, 76% believing in *fengshui*. Yes123.

the two regions to a mutual understanding of the cosmologies and cultural perspectives of the East and West.

An Investigation of Calculation and Destiny
What is destiny?

Civilizations both past and present have been interested in predicting the future and investigating the nature of destiny. Some believe that fate is fixed, while others believe that it can be changed, but can destiny be foreseen? Are there ways, methods, or formulas that allow individuals to predict and even alter their future? In an attempt to take hold of their lives, people in both the East and West have developed many techniques and methodologies to determine their futures in their own cultural and social contexts.

Faced with the many risks of life, how have people from the East and West averted misfortune? Who engages in divinatory activities and how have the results of prognostication and destiny been viewed? What is the cultural significance of the ancient practice of divination in contemporary society?

These questions are asked by the curators of this exhibition. As the title "Calculating × Destiny: Divination in Europe and Taiwan" suggests, the exhibition focuses on two core ideas of divination: calculation and destiny. Here, "calculation" refers to the methods and techniques of inference in divination, while "destiny" points to the concept of fate and the cosmology reflected in the customs of divination. Through the objects used in the practice of divination, this exhibition presents the course of cultural development in the East and West, the concepts of life and death, and the worldviews of Europeans and Taiwanese, rather than the minutiae of divination techniques themselves.

Exotic cultures offer a sense of novelty. This exhibition, therefore, faces the challenge of helping the audience, which consists of people who are mostly strangers to European culture, to easily understand and identify with foreign customs. The exhibition employs the common ground of divination between the East and West, therefore, as the foundation for communication. The exhibition consists of six chapters: Destiny and Fortune; Observation and Calculation; Spiritual Guidance; Changing One's Destiny; Fortune-Telling and Hearing; and Divinations and Games. As they compare objects of divination from Europe and Taiwan and contrast their cultures, which are presented in conjunction with videos, music, and interactive devices, Taiwanese visitors will be able to better understand their own divination culture and to appreciate the treasures of their native culture.

East Meets West

The differences between the objects of divination from the East and West are at the core of the narratives of the subthemes in this exhibition. We have selected items that can be compared or that reverberate with one another, including natal charts, chiromancy illustrations, oracle texts, and talismans, allowing the audience to explore commonalities and divergences between Eastern and Western divination practices. Almanacs (calendars) and talismans are prime examples that show how the East and West developed their own divination cultures with similar prognostication methods.

1.Almanacs (Calendars)

In terms of natural phenomena, the movement of the stars in the sky has been a major occupation of both Eastern and Western civilizations, leading to the development of calendar calculations and astronomies and the appearance of almanacs (farmer's calendars) in different cultures. These timetables of propitious times for life events often served as a reference for both people in both the East and West.

Calendar Chart for 1951
Bigger picture on page 68 to 69. Collection of the NMTH

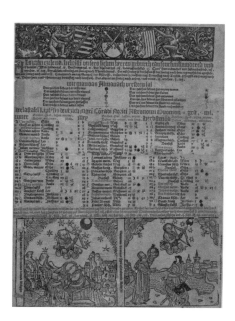

Calendar for 1509
Please check the bigger picture on page 72.
Collection of the
Germanisches Nationalmuseum

Farmer's Calendar for 1624 or 1630
Please check the bigger picture on page 73.
Collection of the Germanisches
Nationalmuseum

The "Calendar Chart for 1951" from Taiwan provided information about the 24 solar terms, the locations of the Fetus God (*Tai-shen*), and the fortuitous dates for starting a business, worshiping, traveling, holding funerals, installing a kitchen, groundbreaking, moving house, visiting the sick, holding weddings, placing a bed, and planting. The "Calendar for 1509" and the "Farmer's Calendar for 1624 or 1630"—both calendars from medieval Europe—marked the Catholic calendar of saints, lunar phases, and auspicious times for bathing, weaning infants, and sowing. These calendars present the concerns of Eastern and Western people—Taiwanese emphasized the correct timing of every aspect of life, while Europeans emphasized links between the conditions of the body and the movement of the stars, such that medical actions, like bloodletting and taking medicines, would be performed in accordance with astrology. The concerns of life reflected the cultures of the East and West.

2.Talismans

Taiwan and Europe share some practices for warding off evil and seeking good fortune, such as wearing amulets or talismans. In Taiwan, talismans for safety, healing, and preventing premature birth were often seen in Taoism-influenced Han Chinese societies, while in Europe, talismans were usually made with parts of animals or vegetables or with gems. Notably, talismans to treat sickness were seen in both the pan-Chinese world and in Europe. For example, in Europe from the 18th to the 20th century, people would buy "Schluckbildchen" ("swallowable pictures"), paper talismans printed with sacred images, at pilgrimage sites. Though some would simply carry them around, others would dissolve them in water before adding them to food to give to sick children or animals. As a "medical" treatment, Schluckbildchen were a rare example of the practice of (almost) magic permitted by the Catholic Church.

**A Printed Five *Wangye*
Safety Talisman from
Nankunshen Temple**
Collection of the NMTH

**The Three Ladies
Malefic Slaying
and Healing Talisman**
Collection of the NMTH

Schluckbildchen
Collection of the Germanisches
Nationalmuseum

**Amulet Cards with Magical
Characters and Words**
Collection of the Germanisches
Nationalmuseum

After the Telling

The most-asked follow-up question to the practice of fortunetelling is probably "Does it really work?" While many people consider fortunetelling an important consideration point in the choices they make, others might never consider having their fortunes told. Is divination a superstition, or does it really serve as a beacon in life? Today, the answers to this question are more diverse than ever before.

Thanks to technology and advances in international travel, divination cultures in different regions have spread and interacted worldwide, making fortunetelling practices even more diverse. Introduced in Taiwan in the late 1980s, tarot cards and Western astrology have only become icebreakers at social events, they have also become favorite divination methods with young people. Taiwanese cartoon artists, including Su-lan Yu, Der-Jen, and Selena Lin, have adapted their creations for tarot cards, establishing a homegrown tarot card industry in Taiwan. The popularization and gamification of divination texts, along with trends in fortunetelling promoted by print media, television programs, and internet videos, have also played crucial roles in nudging divination in Taiwan toward modernity, commercialization, and entertainment [02].

Digital tools have helped to change the way people think about divination. Because of digital technology, divinatory reading is no longer a monopoly of diviners. Now, people can easily turn to fortunetelling websites to quickly find answers for themselves. The results of such predictions are even posted to social media, such as Facebook or Instagram, as a way to express one's personality or inner self. In contemporary Taiwan, divination is not simply about predicting the future. It is also therapeutic and is used to seek self-identity and meaning in life.

I hope that you enjoy this exhibition and that, perhaps, divination can help point your life in the right direction.

---

[02] Jiang-ying, Lee. (2015). Xiao Xiang's divination practices and his physiognomy (1976–2014), pp.62-74. [Master's thesis, Department of History, National Taiwan Normal University].

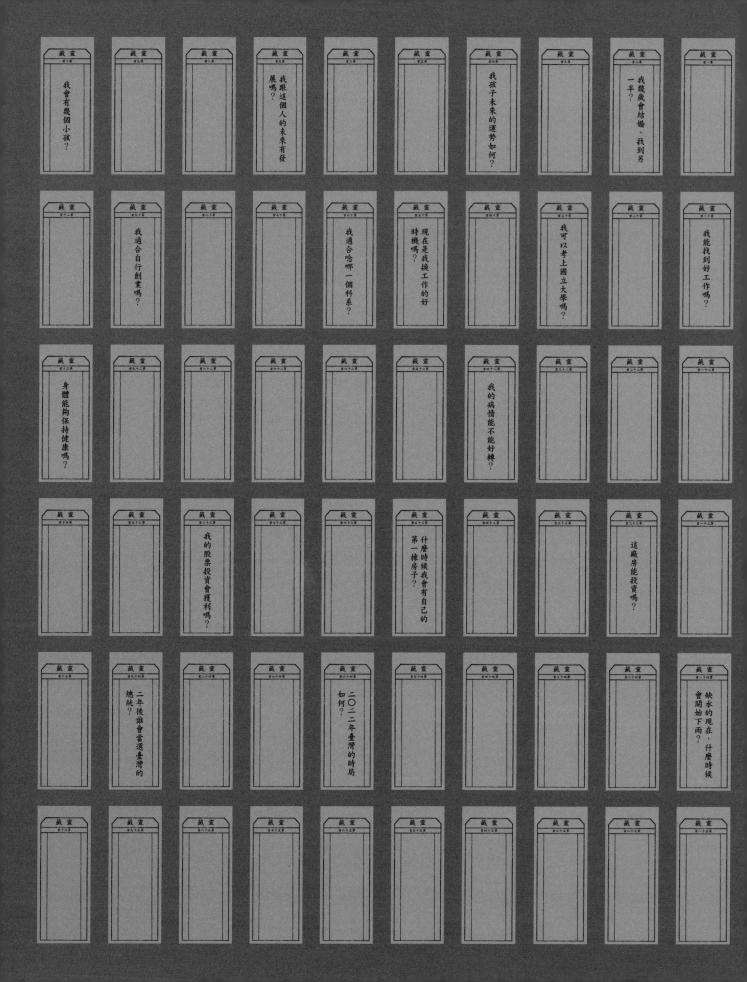

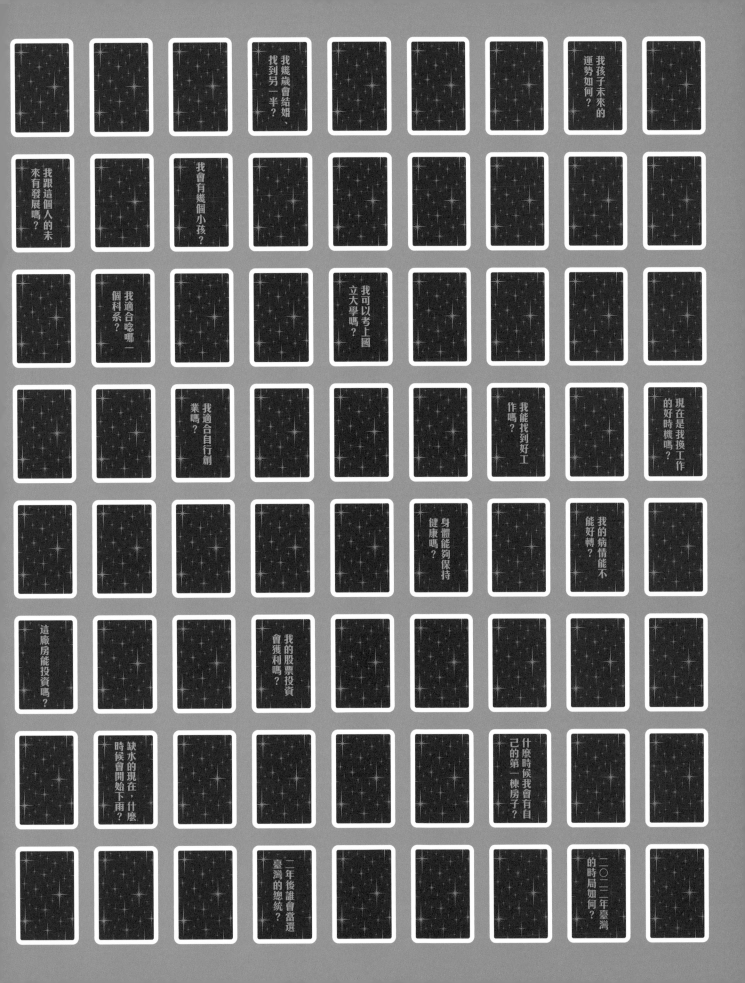

01 命與運

Destiny and Fortune
Vorherbestimmung und Schicksal

命運是千百年以來人們好奇、不斷探索的課題。阿吉仔的〈命運的吉他〉與旺福樂團的〈一人一半〉唱出「為什麼比別人較歹命」、「一人一命 沒人相同；有好命人 有歹命人」，似乎「好命歹命天註定」。人的命運真的早已決定？命運能改變嗎？為了掌握「命運」，改變未來，人們發展各種占卜方法，試圖藉由超自然的力量，解答愛情、婚姻、生子、學業、工作、功名、財富、健康、人際關係…等與個人切身相關的問題。占卜作為日常生活的一部分，因著不同文化、社會、時代、階層的人群而有著不同的意義與風貌。本特展藉由占卜文物，展現占卜的參與者與世界觀，邀請觀眾思考占卜的文化意涵。

✖

Destiny and fortune are subjects that people have contemplated and explored for thousands of years. In his song *Destiny's Guitar*, Taiwanese singer Ajizai laments, "Why am I the unfortunate one?" and in their tune *You Complete me*, the band Won Fu sang, "Each person has one life and each life is different, some good, some bad," as if our lives were predetermined. But are our futures really predetermined? Can we change the course of our lives? To gain insight into one's "fate" and perhaps seek to recast one's future, various methods of fortune-telling have developed over the centuries that have sought to tap the power of the supernatural to solve personal matters, including love, marriage, fertility, study, career, renown, wealth, health, and all forms of interpersonal relationships. A part of everyday life, fortune telling has developed in numerous forms and taken on different significance in various cultures, societies, eras, and social classes. Through the objects of divination, this exhibition aims to take the audience on a journey to divine the cultural implications of fortune telling, reveal its participants, and unveil the cosmology of prophecy.

Das Schicksal ist ein Thema, das die Menschen schon seit Jahrtausenden fasziniert und zu seiner stetigen Erkundung antreibt. In A Chis "Gitarre des Schicksals" und Won Fus "Ein Mensch, eine Hälfte" fallen Zeilen wie "Warum ist mein Schicksal schlechter als das der Anderen", "Jeder Mensch hat sein Schicksal, und keines davon ist gleich; es gibt Menschen mit gutem Schicksal und Menschen mit schlechtem Schicksal", so als ob "gutes und schlechtes Schicksal vom Himmel vorbestimmt sind". Ist das Schicksal eines Menschen tatsächlich schon längst vorherbestimmt? Kann sich das Schicksal ändern? Um das Schicksal zu kontrollieren und die Zukunft zu ändern, haben die Menschen verschiedenste Methoden des Wahrsagens entwickelt, um zu versuchen, mithilfe übernatürlicher Kräfte Fragen über sie persönlich direkt betreffende Fragen über Themen wie Liebe, Heirat, Kindsgeburt, Schulbildung, Arbeit, Reputation, Wohlstand, Gesundheit, zwischenmenschliche Beziehungen und vieles weitere zu beantworten. Die Wahrsagung ist ein Teil des alltäglichen Lebens und hat aufgrund von Faktoren wie verschiedener Kulturen, Gesellschaften, Zeitaltern und Gesellschaftsschichten bei verschiedenen Menschen unterschiedliche Bedeutungen und Erscheinungsformen. Diese Sonderausstellung lädt die Betrachter dazu ein, anhand von Artefakten, welche die Teilnehmer der Wahrsagung und deren Weltsichten aufzeigen, über deren kulturellen Gehalt nachzudenken.

算 × 命

歐洲與臺灣的
占卜特展

Vorhersagen × Schicksal

Wahrsagen in Europa und Taiwan

命與運

命運是千百年以來人們好奇、不斷探索的課題。阿吉仔的〈命運的吉普〉與旺福樂團的〈一人一半〉唱出「為什麼比別人較歹命」、「一人一命 沒人相同；有好命人 有歹命人」，似乎「好命歹命天注定」，人的命運真的早已決定？命運能改變嗎？為了瞭解「命運」改變未來，人們發展各種占卜方法，試圖藉由超自然的力量，解答愛情、婚姻、生子、學業、工作、功名、財富、健康、人際關係...等與個人切身相關的問題。占卜作為日常生活的一部分，因著不同文化、社會、時代、階層的人群而有著不同的意義與風貌。本特展藉由占卜文物，展現占卜的參與者與世界觀，邀請觀眾思考占卜的文化意涵。

Destiny and Fortune

Destiny and fortune are subjects that people have contemplated and explored for thousands of years. In his song Destiny's Guitar, Taiwanese singer A-ji-zai laments, "Why am I the unfortunate one?" and in their tune You Complete Me, the band Won Fu sang, "Each person has one life and each life is different, some good, some bad," reflect the belief that our lives are predetermined by destiny.

But are our futures predetermined? Can we change the course of our lives? To gain insight into one's "destiny" and perhaps seek to reroute one's future, various methods of divination have developed over the centuries that have sought to tap the power of the supernatural to solve personal matters, including love, marriage, fertility, study, career, renown, wealth, health, and all forms of interpersonal relationships. A part of everyday life, fortune telling has developed in numerous forms and taken on different significance in various cultures, societies, eras, and social classes. Through the objects of divination, this exhibition aims to take the audience on a journey to discover the cultural implications of fortune telling, reveal its participants, and unveil the cosmology of prophecy.

Vorherbestimmung und Schicksal

Das Schicksal ist ein Thema, das die Menschen schon seit Jahrtausenden beschäftigt...

02

觀察與推算
Observation and Calculation
Beobachtung und Berechnung

占卜經常觀察與推算並用。例如歐洲、東亞皆有的占星術、紫微斗數等，屬於依術推算。東亞華人社會比較特殊的則是相地的風水術、相法、米占等則屬觀察類的卜術。

✖

Divination often involves observation and calculation. For example, astrology in Europe and *ziwei doushu*, often referred to as Purple Star Astrology, in East Asia are forms of fortune-telling used to deduce one's destiny. Rice divining, physiognomy, and *fengshui*—the "reading" of a place—, fortune-telling methods that are more prevalent in Chinese communities in East Asia, tend to rely more on observation.

✖

Die Wahrsagung nutzt oft sowohl Beobachtung als auch Berechnung. So zählen beispielsweise die sowohl in Europa als auch Ostasien verbreiteten Systeme wie etwa die westliche sowie die chinesische Purpurstern-Astrologie zu den Berechnungskünsten. Die in Ostasien unter ethnischen Chinesen verbreiteten und eher speziellen geomantischen Methoden wie Feng-Shui, Gesichtslesekunst und Reisorakel dagegen gehören zu den auf Beobachtung basierenden Wahrsagekünsten.

自然現象
Natural Phenomena
Natürliche Phänomene

觀察自然現象是人類文明中常見的占法。例如：突然出現大批蜈蚣，可能是地震的前兆；出現紅色月亮，可能會發生災難；聽到烏鴉的叫聲是不祥之兆。經由觀察星象、地形、地震、溪水清濁、極光、閃電、日蝕、星象變化、動物出現奇怪的行為，或是植物的生長違反時令等大自然的變化，是很古老的占卜方法。其中有些有經驗依據，有些則建立在天人感應的思想上。

觀察自然，以預測未來最為人所熟知的是星占，用以預測個人或是國家的命運。歐洲生辰占星學的出生圖與中國傳統八字算命的命盤，都是這一系的數術。現今東亞人們普遍使用的農民曆，受到清代官方的《時憲書》影響。這原是由天主教傳教士引進歐洲天文學所改的曆法，但為了適應國情，他們也不得不保留農民曆的舖注形式，見證了曆占的東西文化交流。

Observing natural phenomena is a common divination practice across different civilizations. The emergence of legions of centipedes may be a sign of an earthquake; a blood moon could bode a coming catastrophe; and the cawing of crows might be considered an ominous omen. Interpreting the stars, landscape, earth tremors, the clarity of rivers, auroras, lightning, solar eclipses, and unusual animal behavior, are among the most ancient divination methods known. While some interpretations may have empirical foundations, others are based on theories of supernatural sensitivity or "correspondence between heaven and mankind."

One of the most popular ways of predicting the future through observing nature is astrology. It is used for both people and nations. The horoscope in European astrology and the birth chart of the traditional Chinese Four Pillars of Destiny are calculative divination systems based on knowledge of celestial mechanics. The calendrical divinations of the East and West also have their moments of cultural exchange: the almanac commonly used in East Asia today was adapted from *Shixianlis* (Timely modelling Calendar) issued during the Qing era, which was a revision of European astronomy by Catholic missionaries, but with traditional Chinese notations to meet the needs of choosing an auspicious date.

隋書曰

暴兵氣

凡敵上有黑雲來臨我軍上彼兵欲襲我也宜急防備之不

可輕戰

宋志曰

黑雲從敵上來之我軍上敵人告發欲來襲我宜備不宜戰

天色蒼芒而有此氣依日干支數內無風雨則所發之方必

有暴兵日尅時則凶特尅日則自消散

天文象占
Divinations by Astrological and Meteorological Phenomena

推測編印於南宋末年或明代的《天文象占》，是觀測天文氣象的預測書。中研院藏本存有〈雲氣出入三垣說〉、〈軍中侯氣說〉2卷，先圖後文。〈軍中侯氣說〉分析了猛將氣、賢將氣、暴兵氣、伏兵氣……等47種雲氣所反映的徵兆，作為用兵制敵的參考。

中央研究院歷史語言研究所傅斯年圖書館　藏

瓦爾代克城堡神蹟

Miraculous Sign over Waldeck Castle

自 16 世紀中後期開始，歐洲人普遍認為世界末日將至，神
會透過特殊的自然現象給予預兆。本件呈現 1554 年在德國
南部的瓦爾代克城堡上方觀察到北極光奇觀，畫有 2 個手
持火劍的武士打鬥的場景，象徵著三十年戰爭的激烈戰場。

日耳曼國家博物館 藏
Germanisches Nationalmuseum, Nuremberg, Germany

立石鐵臣繪《日食龍山寺》
Solar Eclipse Over Longshang Temple
Painted by Tateishi Tetsuomi

天狗食日的現象，常常被視為不祥之兆。1941 年 9 月 21 日臺北發生日食天文奇觀，引起觀測熱潮。立石鐵臣以版畫記錄下當時人們的反應，描繪萬華龍山寺的一名黑衣白髮老婦面向太陽持香、跪拜。

《民俗臺灣》第 1 卷 5 號，1941 年 11 月，頁 31。
南天書局 提供

日食艋舺風俗
Customs of Solar Eclipse at Monga

臺灣民間傳說日食是太陽預知世間將流行惡疫，所以代替眾生而生病，因此人們須在此時拜拜、放鞭炮、鳴鼓、誦經祈禱，直到太陽恢復正常為止。圖像為松山虔三拍攝 1941 年 9 月 21 日臺北萬華日食發生時常民的景象。

《民俗臺灣》第 1 卷 6 號，1941 年 12 月，頁 30-31。
國立臺灣歷史博物館 藏
2019.031.1040

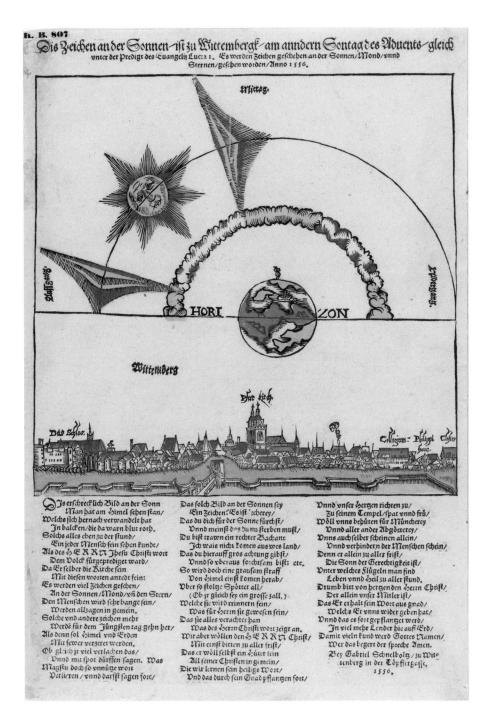

威登堡上空的光環
Halo over Wittenberg

本件報導了 1556 年為了準備慶祝耶穌聖誕的將臨節第 2 個星期日禮拜
時觀察到的日食現象，就在牧師宣講《路加福音》世界末日經文之時。

日耳曼國家博物館 藏
Germanisches Nationalmuseum, Nuremberg, Germany

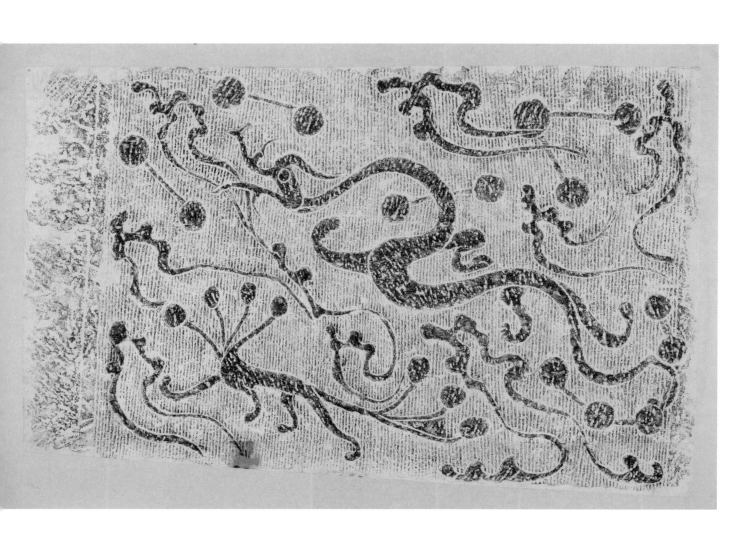

星象神獸圖
Stars and Divine Animals

中國古代常將天文觀測結果與星占、術數結合，
成為高度政治化的天文知識。本件東漢時期的南
陽漢畫星象神獸圖拓本，為東方的蒼龍星座，龍
身被14顆星所環繞，左下有一四足三尾的神獸。

中央研究院歷史語言研究所傅斯年圖書館　藏

星盤
Astrolabe

星盤是歐洲中世紀主要的天文儀器，具有觀測、
計時、計算與預測等功能。本件具有 16 世紀下
半葉活躍於比利時魯汶的星盤製造師阿森紐斯
（Gualterus Arsenius）作品的精美華麗特徵，於
16 世紀下半至 1715 年間製造，正面尺規已不見。

日耳曼國家博物館 藏
Germanisches Nationalmuseum, Nuremberg, Germany

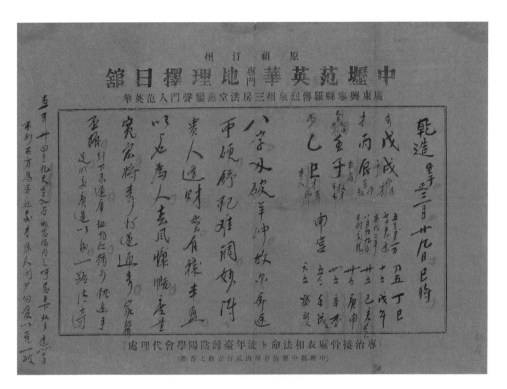

中壢范英華專門地理擇日館批命命書
Chinese Horoscope

昭和時期中壢范英華專門地理擇日館替一男子推算其流年與大運。命書上方特別標記范英華祖籍汀州，為廣東興寧縣羅傳烈、泉州三房洪堂燕鑾聲門人，意指該擇日館融通了泉州繼成堂洪潮和通書及廣東興寧羅家通書二家之說。

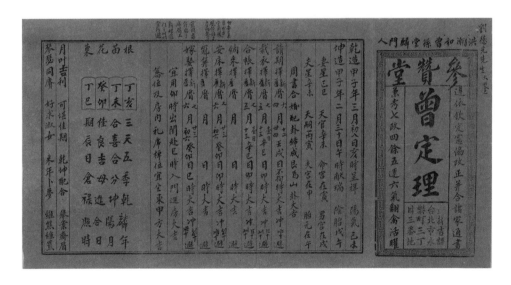

參贊堂曾定理嫁娶吉課
Wedding Horoscope

昭和時期臺北市擇日師曾定理所選之嫁娶吉課，推測是替劉德光先生的兒子或女兒，依男女生辰八字選擇適合辦理納采、安床、嫁娶等喜事之良辰吉時。

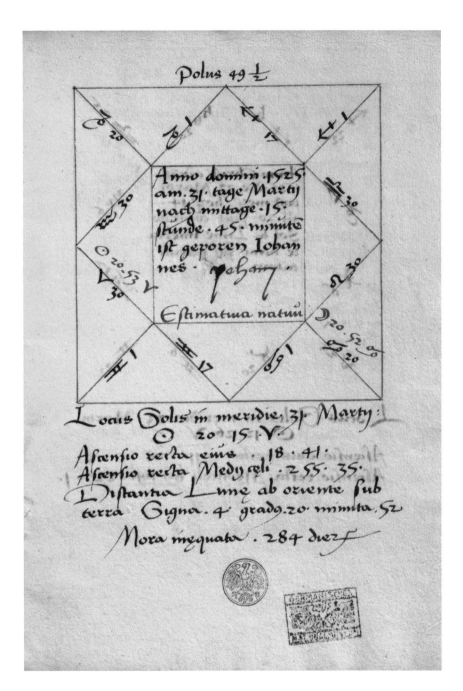

約翰內斯 · 倍海姆的出生圖
Natal Chart for Johannes Behaim

出生圖（本命星盤）特別流行於 16-17 世紀歐洲的上層社會，被作為貴重的禮物。約翰內斯 · 倍海姆（Johannes Behaim）是 1525 年出生於紐倫堡的貴族，其出生圖為早期的方形，與現今常見的圓形不同。占星師依據他的出生時間與地點，計算出太陽、月亮、水星…等十大行星在黃道十二宮的位置，推測他的未來富有、受君主重用，但實際上他可能未成年就過世。

日耳曼國家博物館 藏
Germanisches Nationalmuseum, Nuremberg, Germany

國泰民安

新華戲院街面　　局書印林竹

1951 年春牛圖曆表
Calendar Chart for 1951

民間曆書常見有簡版的單張曆表，列有月份和節氣，以及春牛芒神圖，供一般民眾便於張貼於壁。本件春牛圖由聚福堂擇日館呂逢元編、新竹竹林印書局出版，內容包括年度陰陽曆對照表、流年利方圖、春牛圖、生肖年齡對照圖、符咒等，等同於簡易通書。

國立臺灣歷史博物館　藏
2005.008.1751

《昭和五年臺灣民曆》
Showa Year 5 Taiwan Folk Calendar

日本統治臺灣後，將日本官曆《神宮曆》引進臺灣，於 1914-
1945 年由臺灣總督府主導編印、臺灣神苑會發行《臺灣民曆》，
採用太陽曆曆法，具有神宮曆內容的天文星象、二十四節氣、
天皇年表、祝祭日等內容，與常民生活作息呈現重大隔閡。

國立臺灣歷史博物館 藏
2005.008.1690

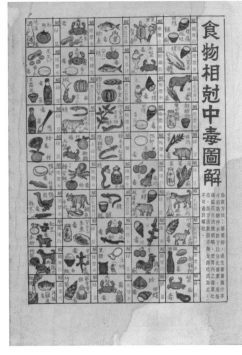

《1994 年臺灣農民曆》
Chinese Calendar for 1994

臺北呂逢元地理擇日館編製，竹林書局發行。

國立臺灣歷史博物館 藏／李道明捐贈
2001.013.0068

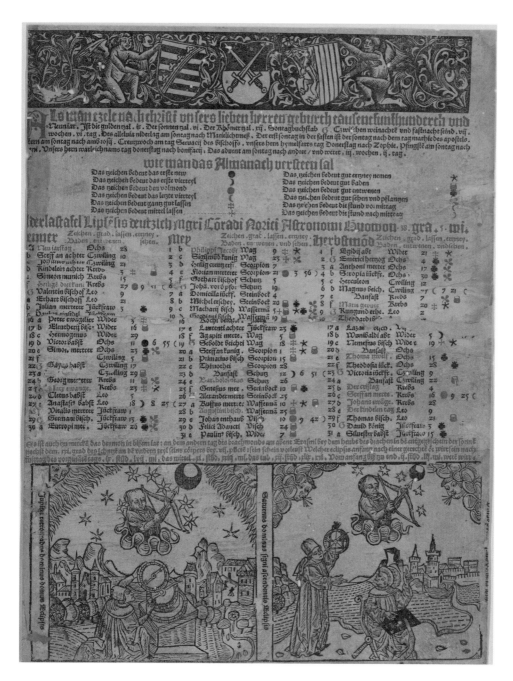

1509 年年曆

Calendar for the Year 1509

近現代歐洲許多年曆編撰者為醫師，本件即集醫師、數學家、天文學家身份的康拉德 · 托克勒（Conrad Tockler，1470-1530）編撰之年曆。中間為年曆表，月份可能為 1、5、9 月，標示有聖人日、月相及適合放血、服藥、洗澡、斷奶、播種的時間；最下方 2 張插圖，呈現出日食及星體的觀測，由天文學家（左圖）與醫師（右圖）分別操作星盤的景象。

日耳曼國家博物館 藏
Germanisches Nationalmuseum, Nuremberg, Germany

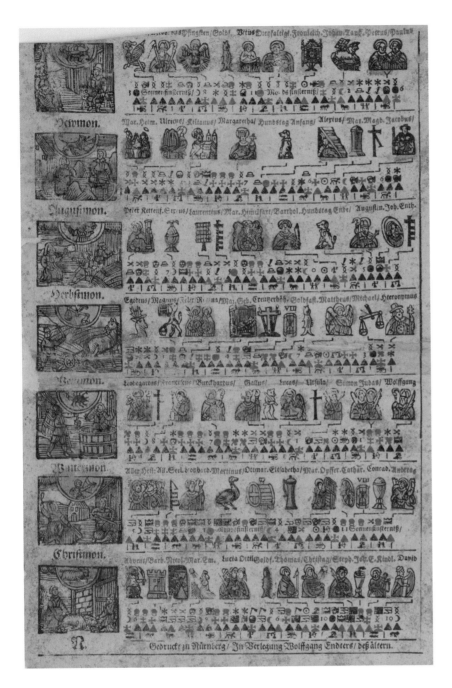

1624 年或 1630 年農民曆
Farmer's Calendar for 1624 or 1630

印刷術的普及，使得歐洲占卜文本大量出現，常見為占星掛曆及年曆。掛曆是記載有關教會節日、聖人日、適合播種、占星吉日等重要日子的指南。本件左側圖繪有 6-12 月黃道十二宮之巨蟹宮至魔羯宮的每月農村勞動生活場景。右側日曆圖示以黑色三角形代表平日、紅色為周日。最上方為聖人日等符號，例如 11 月 25 日上有輪子符號，象徵聖凱薩琳（St. Catherine of Alexandria）被死亡輪行刑之意，即為「聖凱薩琳日」。

日耳曼國家博物館 藏
Germanisches Nationalmuseum, Nuremberg, Germany

占星適合洗澡、斷奶、
播種時間圖
Astrologically Favorable
Times for Bathing, Baby
Weaning, and Sowing

16-17 世紀是歐洲占卜的黃金時
代，占卜的面向更貼近於常民生
活。放血、服藥、洗澡、斷奶、
播種等生活行事曆，常刊印於年
曆。本件印刷於 1495-1505 年，
圖形似星盤，圓心為洗澡、斷奶、
播種等 3 個生活場景，最外圈為
黃道十二宮，場景圖標有星座代
號字母，代表適合執行的時間。

日耳曼國家博物館 藏
Germanisches Nationalmuseum,
Nuremberg, Germany

放血人體圖
Anatomical Figure of the
"Bloodletting Man"

放血人體圖，被用於歐洲的占星
醫療學，圖解標示出人體與黃道
十二宮對應的特定部位，例如頭
部對應的是牡羊座，肩膀、手為
雙子座，當月亮進入支配身體部
位主管的星座時，避免放血。本
件製作於 15 世紀末。

日耳曼國家博物館 藏
Germanisches Nationalmuseum,
Nuremberg, Germany

放血刀
Phlebotomy Knife in a Wooden Case

溼式拔罐即為拔罐放血，利用特殊的刀片，在患處的皮膚上切開一些小傷口，讓血流入拔罐杯內，藉以排毒、淨化身體。一般人會選擇在年曆標示的放血吉日進行。本件製作於 17-18 世紀。

日耳曼國家博物館 藏
Germanisches
Nationalmuseum,
Nuremberg, Germany

拔罐杯
Cupping Glasses

19 世紀歐洲人們習慣到鄉村小鎮找一家歷史悠久的理髮店，進行桑拿與拔罐療法，放鬆身體，當時的理髮師也兼職替人進行放血、開刀等外科醫療。歐洲的拔罐分為乾、溼二種，乾式即為「拔火罐」，以火加熱罐子，產生真空的壓力，吸附在特定部位的皮膚上，舒緩緊張和疼痛。本件製作於 18 世紀。

日耳曼國家博物館 藏
Germanisches Nationalmuseum, Nuremberg, Germany

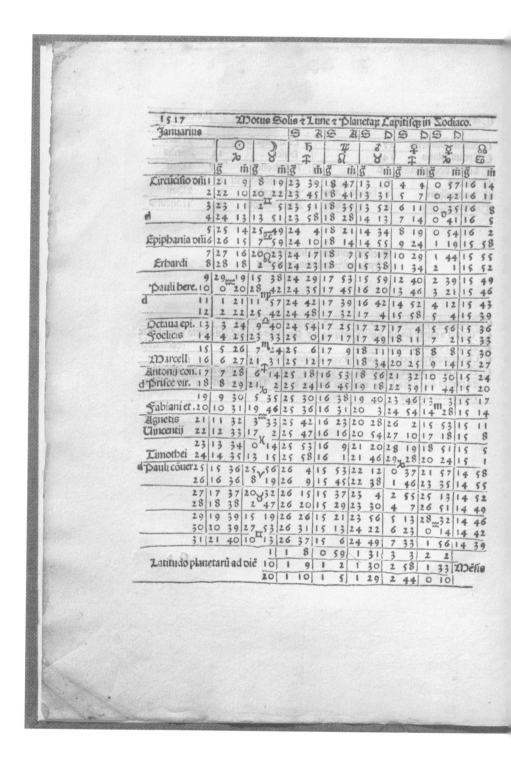

星曆表

Ephemeris

星曆表出現之後，更精確預測星體的位置，使得星盤在占卜實踐變得邊緣化。本件為德國 15-16 世紀的數學家、天文學家、占星家約翰內斯・斯托夫勒（Johannes Stöffler，1452-1531）製作 1504-1526 年之星曆表，刊載每天太陽、月亮、行星、慧星的計算位置數據表列，可供占星及天文使用。

日耳曼國家博物館 藏
Germanisches Nationalmuseum, Nuremberg, Germany

an.	☉	♄ or	♃ or	♂ oc	♀ or	☿ or	Solis et plax i ter ſe.
			□ 21	♂ 10			
	△ 4						
		☌ 21	✳ 9		☍ 9		
			✳ 14		☍ 10	☽ ♌	
	☍ 14 30				△ 18		
		△ 16	♂ 4	□ 1		△ 9	
	△ 12	□ 22		△ 8	□ 5	□ 17	
			✳ 13		✳ 14		□ ♃ ♂ △ ♃ ♀
	□ 20 32	✳ 3		□ 16	☍ 19	✳ 1	
	✳ 2		△ 17			♂ 3	
		♂ 7				♂ 14	
			△ 1			☽ ♉	
	♂ 15 19	✳ 16	☍ 23	□ 7	✳ 20	♂ ♄ ♀	
			✳ 17		✳ 15		
	✳ 18	□ 0	△ 14	□ 10		☍ ☉ ♃ △ ♂ ☿	
		△ 11		△ 3	□ 11		
	□ 8 55		□ 0	♂ 17		△ 5	
		✳ 10					

                  Ω 3

占星醫療儀器
Disc-Shaped Astrological-Medical Instrument

近代是歐洲鐘錶、星盤等儀器製造的多產時期，也是醫學、天文學與占星術緊密關連的時期。當時的醫學認為人類是宇宙的一部分，人體部位會受到行星與恆星的影響，而有某些日子不適合特定的治療。本件為特製的占星醫療儀器，工作原理與星盤相同，透過參考太陽和月亮周期計算治療的時間，由 16 世紀為哈布斯堡王朝工作的精密儀器製造師伊拉斯謨 · 哈伯梅爾（Erasmus Habermehl）在布拉格製造，推測可能為皇帝私人醫生所有。

日耳曼國家博物館 藏
Germanisches Nationalmuseum, Nuremberg, Germany

人體特徵 Physiognomy
Körperliche Besonderheiten

臉國字，官運亨；手掌厚，福氣飽。這些來自人體的訊息，在中國傳統「氣的宇宙觀」之下，認為人生之時，氣之強弱已顯示體相之上，決定了個人未來的命運。因而可以藉由考察身體特徵，得知其運勢。歐洲亦有手相、面相之術。其後也運用在醫學與心理學，探究人的性格、能力與習慣等。其他如眼皮跳雖與相術無關，但人們也常將之視為徵兆。

In Chinese physiognomy, a square face represents a prosperous career as an official, while a thick hand suggests an abundance of good luck. Such interpretations of the human body mark a form of traditional Chinese cosmology in which a person's future is determined by one's *qi*, the strength or weakness of which determines one's destiny and which is already evident on the body at birth. Palm and face readings are also found in European cultures, and these were even extended to medical science and psychology to explain an individual's personality, talents, and habits. Although unrelated to physiognomy, phenomena, like eyelid twitching, are also often regarded as signs, too.

手相八卦十二宮圖
Diagram of the Palm's Eight Directions and Twelve Astrological Houses

《麻衣相法》是流傳最廣的相學經典之作，本書為吳心鏡考訂柳莊麻衣相法之版本。此頁面為手相「八卦十二宮圖」，依周易八卦將手掌分為八個方位、十二宮位，手心為明堂，食指代表主人（自己），無名指則代表客人（妻子）。

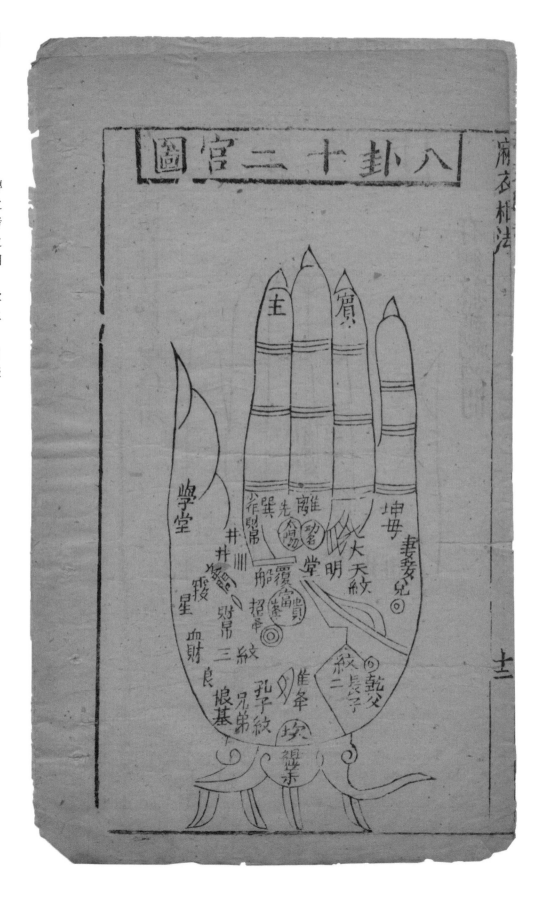

八卦指掌雕版
Printing Plate of the "Jade Hand"

本件為手相「八卦圖」的木刻雕版，背面寫有「己卯年上杭丘天錫置」字樣，推測為1939年購入。

國立臺灣歷史博物館 藏
2003.008.0776

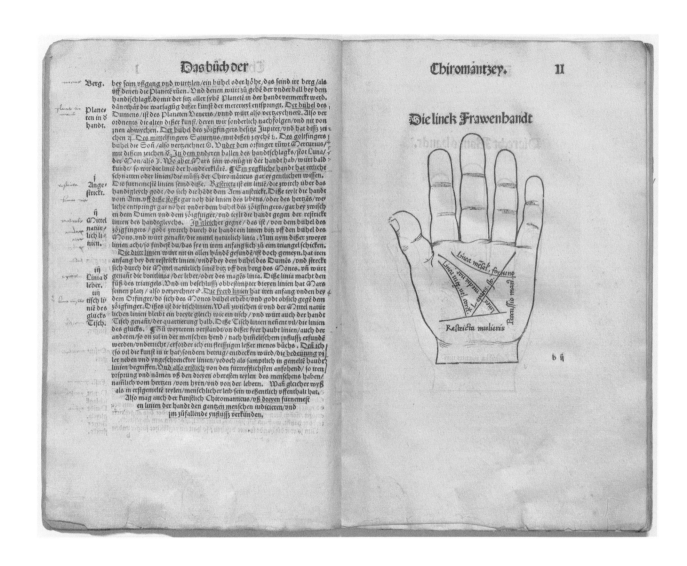

《手相的藝術》
The Art of Chiromancy

德國神學家和占星家約翰內斯·英達金（Johannes Indagine）撰寫的
手相術，是德國著名的手相書，由掌紋線條判斷人的性格與命運，男
性看右手，女性看左手，最初以拉丁文書寫，本書為 1523 年德文譯本。

日耳曼國家博物館 藏
Germanisches Nationalmuseum, Nuremberg, Germany

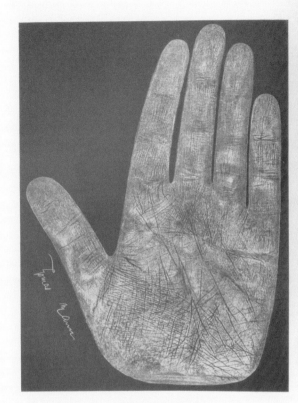

THOMAS MANN

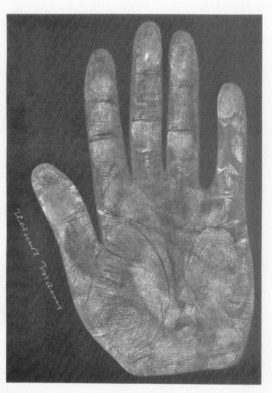

HEINRICH MANN

《手和個性》
Hand and Personality

德國柏林著名的手相師瑪麗安·拉希格（Marianne Raschig）將顧客的手印記錄集結成書，於 1931 年出版《手和個性》。書中她將顧客的手印進行分組比較，試圖找尋其典型的特徵。此二頁面是一對兄弟的掌紋線條比較。

日耳曼國家博物館 藏
Germanisches Nationalmuseum, Nuremberg, Germany

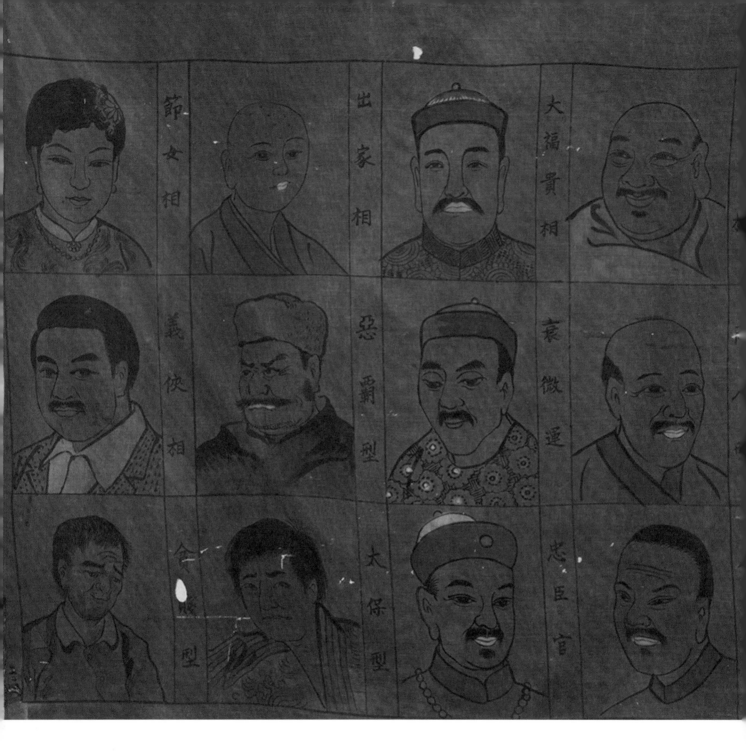

面相圖譜
Diagrams of Physiognomy

據購藏來源指為日本時代臺中地區命相館或算命
攤使用的面相圖譜，繪有 24 種面相，其中女性
只佔 3 種，顯見傳統社會以男性為主的價值觀。

國立臺灣歷史博物館 藏
2018.024.0265

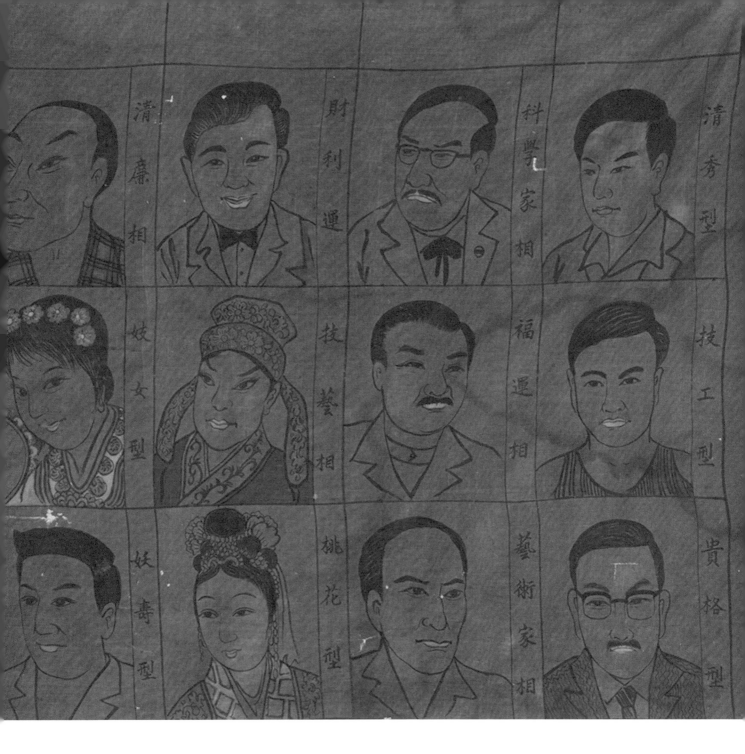

清秀型

科學家相

財利運相

清廉相

技工型

福運相

技藝相

妓女型

貴格型

藝術家相

桃花型

妖壽型

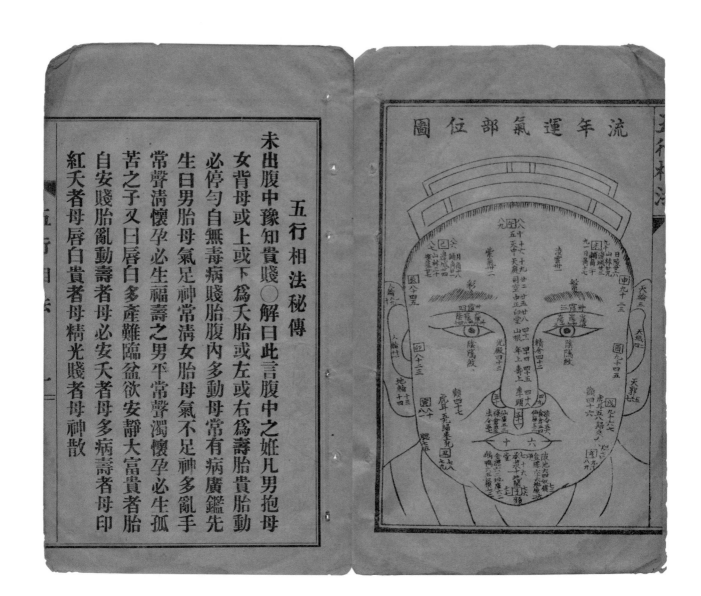

五行相法秘傳

未出腹中豫知貴賤○解曰此言腹中之姙凡男抱母
女背母或上或下爲天胎或左或右爲壽胎貴胎動
必停勻自無毒病賤胎腹內多動母常有病廣鑑先
生曰男胎母氣足神常清女胎母氣不足神多亂手
常聲清懷孕必生福壽之男常聲濁懷孕必生孤
苦之子又曰唇白多產難臨盆欲安靜大富貴者胎
自安賤胎亂動壽者母必安天者母多病壽者母胎
紅天者母唇白貴者母精光賤者母神散

昌仁堂發行《五行相法》
The Five Elements Divination Published by
Changren Tang

昌仁堂 1937 年發行。昌仁堂前身為創立於清道
光年間、府城著名的大書坊松雲軒。

國立臺灣歷史博物館 藏
2006.002.1553

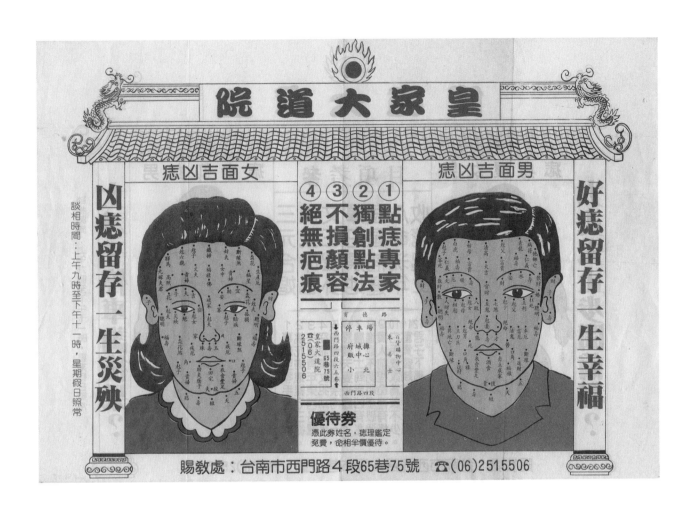

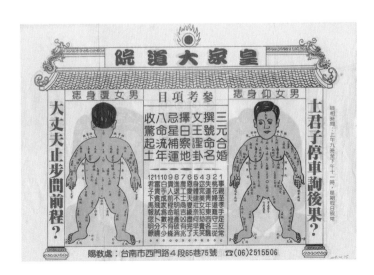

皇家大道院點痣廣告單
Flyer of Huang Jia Da Dao Yuan's Mole
Removal Service

痣相，也是占測吉凶禍福的依據之一。本件為臺南市皇家大道院命相館的點痣廣告單，印有男、女面痣圖，說明痣在不同部位的吉凶意涵，特別強調「好痣留存一生幸福，凶痣留存一生災殃」，痣被視為一種人生命運的符號。

國立臺灣歷史博物館 藏
2018.024.0075

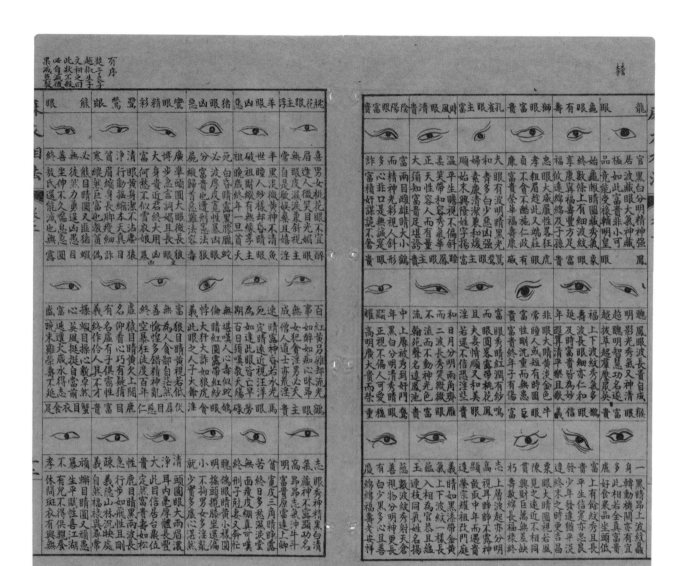

《改良繪圖麻衣神相全編》
Mayi Shen Xiang Quan Bian

《麻衣神相》內容豐富、通俗實用，成為相學代
表之作，除面相外，還包括眉、眼、鼻、口、唇、
舌、耳等之相法。

國立臺灣歷史博物館　藏
2018.024.0135

人為推算 Calculation
Menschliche Berechnung

以紫微斗數看流年運勢、八字合婚、易占、龜卜、米卦、陰陽宅風水、或為商店或出生的小孩取名，這些以推算為基礎的占卜方法，是東亞社會常見的占術。

臺灣術數的發展，除了中國的影響外，也受到日本文化的影響，最明顯的就是筆劃姓名學。臺南命相師白惠文於 1930 年代引進「熊崎式姓名學」，即以五格筆劃的 81 靈動數來判斷姓名的吉凶，成為今日最常見的命名方式。

Approaches based on calculation are also popular fortune-telling methods in East Asian societies. These include reading the year's fortunes using *ziwei doushu*; choosing a marriage partner with the Four Pillars of Destiny; divinations using *Yijing*, tortoiseshells, or rice; creating the right *fengshui* for a house or a tomb; and naming companies and even newborn babies.

Though the development of calculative fortune telling in Taiwan was inherited primarily from China, it has also been influenced by Japanese culture with the stroke count of names being the most notable example. Introduced by the Tainan-based fortune-teller Hui-wen Bai in 1930, the Kumasaki naming system from Japan, which uses the number of strokes of the characters that correspond to the "five cases" (*wuge*) of a name (with a total number of 81) to determine a person's fortune has become one of the most common ways of naming in modern Taiwan.

《監本易經》
Jian Ben Yijing

本件為 1918 年上海鴻文
書局印行之石印版，版本
源自國子監藏書。《易
經》是最古老的占卜之
書，也是中國術數理論的
基礎，以六十四卦的卦象
預知世事變化的吉凶。

國立臺灣歷史博物館 藏
2004.007.0264

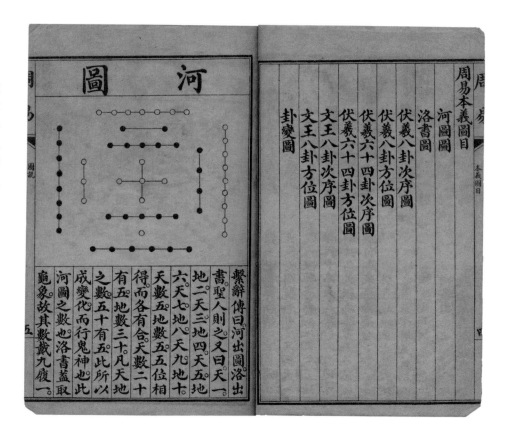

龜卦組
Turtle Shell for *Yijing* Coin Oracle

龜卦的方式是將 3 枚大小相同的銅錢放入烏
龜殼內，搖擲 6 次成卦，據以卜卦問事。銅
錢據說以乾隆通寶卜卦為佳，較具靈力。

秋惠文庫林于昉 提供

羅盤
Fengshui Compass (*Luopan*)

「羅盤」又稱「羅經」，是風水師勘測風水時
必備的工具，也是招財、化煞的法器。構造
上主要由中央天池的指南針及內盤組合而成，
內盤依同心圓一層一層刻製了八卦、二十四天
星、二十四山、節氣、五行等符號。

國立臺灣歷史博物館 藏
2018.024.0234

文公尺兼丁蘭尺
Fengshui Ruler

丁蘭尺用於測量墳墓、祖先牌位等陰宅吉凶，分為財、失、
興、死、官、義、苦、旺、害、丁等十格，一般使用以吉
字為佳。本件為測量陰、陽宅雙用的木尺，一面為文公尺、
一面為丁蘭尺。

國立臺灣歷史博物館 藏
2004.028.0805

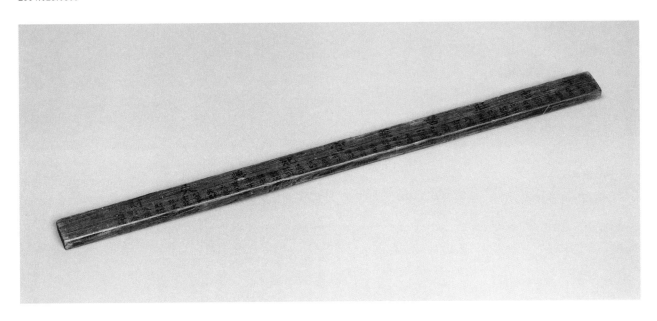

《協象書集造葬論》
Burial Classic

風水，又稱堪輿，是東亞華人社會特有的相地之術，極重地氣，可分為陽宅風水及陰宅風水。本件為張輝新手抄謄寫之《協象書集造葬論》，內容為擇日及造葬的通書，其中「造葬總論」記載了建造墳墓與安葬時須考量五行、墓位坐向方位等。

國立臺灣歷史博物館 藏／蘇進法捐贈
2015.017.0012

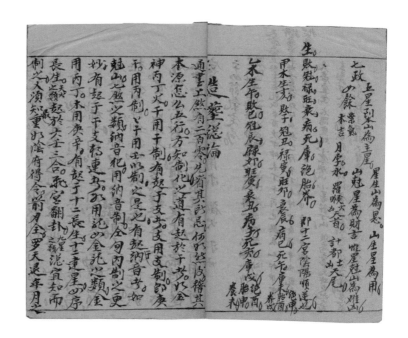

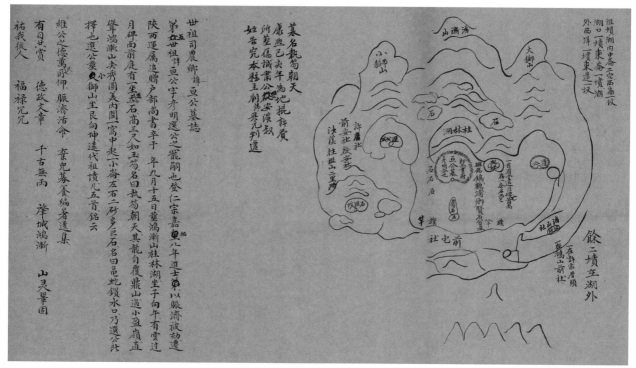

《石氏祠墳考》
Genealogy and Tomb Maps of the Shi Clan (Ding-mei Shi Manor) in Tainan

府城石鼎美、石暘睢家族之祖譜，記載了石氏至清代嘉慶年間之歷代祖先，以及石氏於唐代從西安入福建同安定居後12位祖先之祖墳誌，並繪有祖墳風水穴位圖。此頁面為宋代亘公的介紹及其墓穴圖。

國立臺灣歷史博物館 藏／石允忠捐贈
2013.004.0001.0002

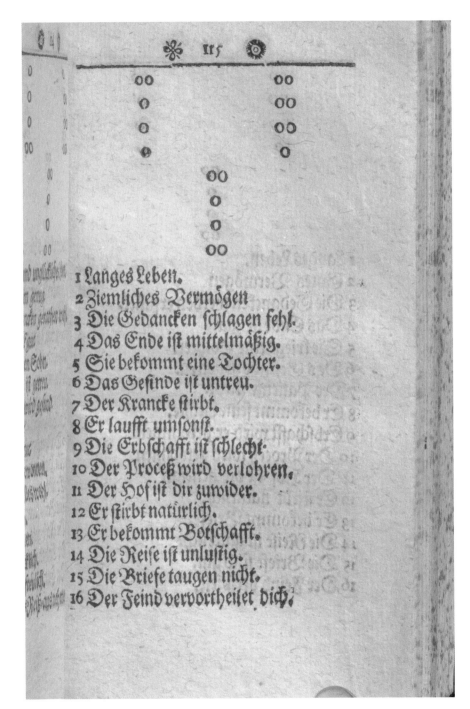

1 Langes Leben.
2 Ziemliches Vermögen.
3 Die Gedancken schlagen fehl.
4 Das Ende ist mittelmäßig.
5 Sie bekommt eine Tochter.
6 Das Gesinde ist untreu.
7 Der Krancke stirbt.
8 Er laufft umsonst.
9 Die Erbschafft ist schlecht.
10 Der Proceß wird verlohren.
11 Der Hof ist dir zuwider.
12 Er stirbt natürlich.
13 Er bekommt Botschafft.
14 Die Reise ist unlustig.
15 Die Briefe taugen nicht.
16 Der Feind vervortheilet dich.

《地占》
Geomantic Judgement Seat

尼古拉斯‧卡塔努斯（Nicolaus Catanus）撰寫、於 1715 年再版有關阿拉伯風水（Geomancy）實踐的書。雖名為「風水」，其實與風水形式無關。地占術，源於北非和阿拉伯伊斯蘭世界的占卜方法，自 12 世紀以來廣為歐洲熟知，阿拉伯語稱為「沙子的科學」，以四行由單點或雙點組合的 15 或 16 個圖形，再由多組圖形構成一張盤，進行預測。

日耳曼國家博物館 藏
Germanisches Nationalmuseum, Nuremberg, Germany

曾天香地理日課店招
**Signboard of the Tian-xiang Tzeng
Geomancy Service**

店招上標記營業項目為八卦占斷、三元合婚。

國立臺灣歷史博物館 藏
2017.015.0167

竹東命理書雕版
**Printing Plate of the Divination Book Circulated in
Eastern Hsinchu**

日本時代竹東地區算命師使用的卜卦命理書雕版，刻有似書卷圖案。

國立臺灣歷史博物館 藏
2017.024.0209

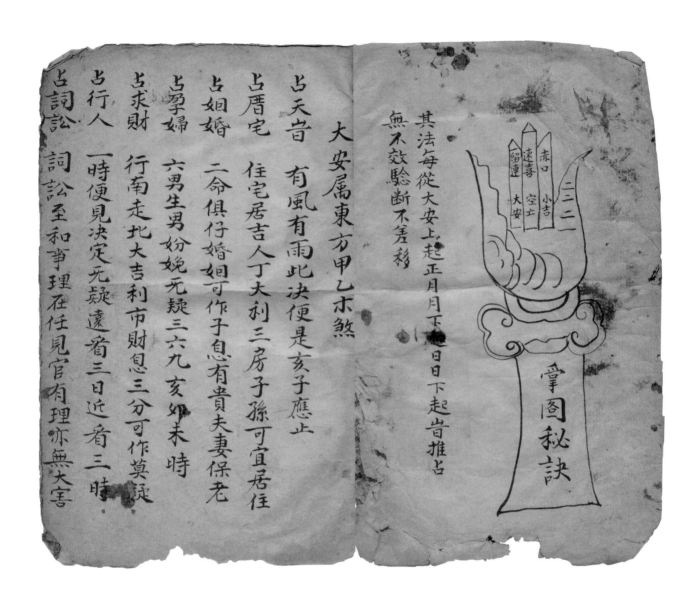

其法每從大安上起正月月下□日日下起當推占

無不效驗斷不差移

掌圖秘訣

赤口　小吉
速喜　空亡
留連　大安

大安屬東方甲乙木煞

占天當　有風有雨此決便是亥子應止

占厝宅　住宅居吉人丁大利三房子孫可宜居住

占姻婚　二命俱仔婚姻可作子息有貴夫妻保老

占孕婦　六男生男妨娩元疑三六九亥卯未時

占求財　行南走北大吉利市財息三分可作莫疑

占行人　一時便見決定元疑遠者三日近者三時

占詞訟　詞訟至和事理在任見官有理亦無大害

《掌圖秘訣》
Secrets of the Palm

六壬時課，是依據陰陽五行的掐指神算掌訣。以
左手的食指、中指、無名指排列出大安、留連、
速喜、赤口、小吉、空亡等 6 種神煞格局，取當
時的月、日、時順序，依順時針掐指神算，推算
天氣、住宅、婚姻、懷孕、求財、遠行、訴訟、
失物、墳墓等吉凶結果。

國立臺灣歷史博物館　藏／蘇進法捐贈
2015.017.0015

1949 年《聚福堂呂逢元通書便覽》
Feng-yuan Lu Tong Shu Almanac for the Year 1949

通書為選擇術之書，由民間術家參考官方曆書改編而成，可分為百科全書式通書與年度通書二大類，用以擇吉避凶。本件為民國 38 年度之《聚福堂呂逢元通書便覽》，屬年度通書，由臺北艋舺聚福堂呂逢元印行，內容涉及祭祀、生活、工商、營建、婚姻、喪葬等日常行事擇日。呂逢元於 1920 年代師承自福建漳州紹安的叔叔呂彰星，學習擇日知識。

———————————

國立臺灣歷史博物館 藏／李道明捐贈
2001.013.0098

1948 年《標準農曆通書》
The Standard Agricultural Tong Shu Almanac for the Year 1948

袁樹珊校勘、上海潤德書局印行之農民曆，附有五福法言、農事占候，以及向袁樹珊以星卜諸詢決疑的問題綱要及費用。袁樹珊，出生於醫卜世家，為民國時期著名的命理學家。

———————————

國立臺灣歷史博物館 藏／呂理政捐贈
2004.053.0004

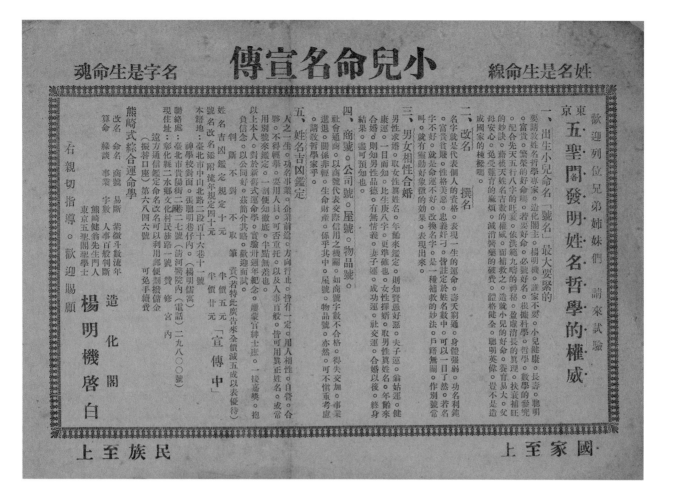

姓名是生命線　小兒命名宣傳　名字是生命魂

楊明機小兒命名宣傳廣告單
Flyer of Ming-ji Yang's Naming Service

楊明機（三芝人，1899-1985）為臺灣鸞堂重要的推手，編修多本鸞書，後來學習日本熊崎健翁之綜合運命學，並以函授方式取得五聖閣學士，為人取名、合婚、看相。

國立臺灣歷史博物館　藏
2011.011.0166

白惠文譯《熊崎式姓名學之神秘》
The Secrets of the Kumasaki Onomancy Translated by Hui-wen Bai

臺灣傳統命名以八字配合五行命名為常見，白惠文（原名白玉光）於1936（昭和11）年將日本改良的姓名學—熊崎健翁姓名學，引進臺灣，翻譯出版《熊崎式姓名學之神秘》一書，姓名學一詞，在臺灣開始風行起來。

白惠文孫　提供

03

神靈的預示
Spiritual Guidance
Göttliche Offenbarung

藉由祖靈、神明、鬼魂等超自然的力量，獲得命運的指示，是占卜另一種方法。不論是希臘、羅馬文化，或是基督教傳統，透過神諭、啟示、先知的預言是歐洲文明中常見的預測未來之術。同樣地，從中國的甲骨文，到一般人就近找大廟以自助的方式求神抽籤、擲筊，或透過乩童、鸞生、尪姨、巫師……等專業人員問事。或臺灣原住民透過與祖靈的互動，取得神明的開示。寺廟等宗教場所，常為人們尋求指引時的地方。

✖

Obtaining guidance for the future through the supernatural powers of ancestor spirits, gods, or ghosts is another approach to divination. In the Greek, Roman, and Christian traditions, oracles, revelations, and prophecies have been the most prevalent forms of prognostication. Similarly, in East Asian societies, people seek answers to issues in their lives through spiritual guidance, from oracle bones in ancient China to "self-help" drawing of fortune sticks, moon-block casting in temples, or from professional spirit mediums, spirit writing, and shamans. Religious institutions may be the most common places for people to seek supernatural guidance, but Taiwanese indigenous people also seek revelations by communing with ancestral spirits.

✖

Eine weitere Methode der Wahrsagung ist das Erlangen von Informationen von übernatürlichen Kräften wie Ahnengeistern, Gottheiten oder Totenseelen. Ganz gleich ob in der griechischen und römischen Kultur oder der christlichen Tradition, sind Voraussagen durch Orakelsprüche, Offenbarungen oder Prophetie in der europäischen Zivilisation eine häufige Methode, die Zukunft zu weissagen. Dies gilt ebenso in China, von den Orakelknochen bis hin zum Besuch von großen Tempeln, wo gewöhnliche Leute eigentätig durch das Ziehen von Losen mit Orakelsprüchen und das Werfen der Halbmondhölzchen, oder aber durch Konsultation eines Trancemediums, eines Praktizierenden des spiritistischen Automatischen Schreibens, eines indigenen Mediums oder anderen rituellen Spezialisten Auskunft über ihre Zukunft erhalten können. Auch taiwanische Ureinwohner erhalten durch Interaktion mit ihren Ahnengeistern Offenbarungen der Götter. Tempel und andere religiöse Stätten sind Orte, an die sich die Menschen häufig richten, wenn sie auf der Suche nach Weisung sind.

直接到廟裡拜拜求籤、擲筊，透過神明開示的籤詩，找到人生的答案，是臺灣普遍使用的占卜方法。除了解答運勢外，生病時求藥籤，以照顧自己或家人的健康。

中國有甲骨的祖先神諭；歐洲則有先知口諭的啟示與預言。例如聖經《但以理書》、《馬太福音》等篇章的記載，尤以「世界末日」的預言最受基督徒所關切。中國的末世預言則有托名於姜子牙的《乾坤萬年歌》、李淳風《推背圖》、劉伯溫《燒餅歌》等三大預言書，其中《燒餅歌》也流通至臺灣，據說也預測了 1895 年臺灣割讓的命運。

夢占在歐洲、東亞雖各自發展，但也因文化情境，而有夢境內容與吉凶預測相當不同。臺灣原住民與打獵相關的夢占故事，或中國大量與科舉相關的夢占故事，便是文化脈絡影響占卜的顯例。

Drawing fortune sticks, casting moon blocks in temples, and using divine lottery poetry are popular divination methods in Taiwan. In addition to seeking guidance in personal matters, many people in Taiwan also ask gods for *yaoqian* (divine medical sticks) to cure themselves or family members.

While China use oracles bones to obtain messages from ancestors, Europe has prophets that give revelations and prophecies. For instance, the eschatological prophecies of the "Book of Daniel" and the "Gospel of Matthew" might be most familiar to Christians. The three books of eschatological prophecies best known in China are Ziya Jiang's *Song of the Universe*, Chunfeng Li's *Tuibeitu*, and Bowen Liu's *Shaobing Song*. Of these Chinese prophetic writings, the *Shaobing Song* is also used in Taiwan as it is believed to have predicted Taiwan being ceded to Japan in 1895.

Oneiromancy—divination based on dreams—has also seen diverse development in both Europe and East Asia, and the cultural context is the decisive factor in what dreams mean and how they are interpreted. In Taiwanese indigenous culture, it is common to see dreams about hunting, while in ancient China, oneirocritic records often involve stories of imperial examinations, illustrating how cultural factors influence the content of divinations.

木雕天上聖母與千里眼順風耳像組
Carved Wooden Statues of Mazu (the Heavenly
Mother) and Qianliyan (the All-Seeing) and
Shunfeng'er (the All-Hearing)

媽祖為臺灣人普遍信仰的神祇。本組天上聖母與千順將
軍像,為清代官祀媽祖廟奉祀,千里眼及順風耳做著官
袍、皂靴、戴官帽造型。

國立臺灣歷史博物館 藏/楊恭熙與黃勻秋捐贈
2017.001.0221

籤筒及籤
Lottery Tube and Sticks

臺灣的籤筒形式，依手持、置於桌面或地上等使用需求有不同的高度，常見的造型為圓型、六角型、八角型等。籤枝順序編號，則以數字及天干為常見。圖中的大觀音亭籤筒組（第2排左）為1972年製作，屬落地八角造型。

國立臺灣歷史博物館 藏
2003.001.0988、2003.001.0989
2004.025.0971、2004.025.0972
2017.001.1878

筊杯組
Divination Blocks
("Moon Blocks")

筊杯依材質主要分為竹製、木製，也有各種的大小尺寸。

國立臺灣歷史博物館 藏
2003.001.0579、2003.001.0580
2003.001.0583、2003.001.0584

黃金田繪《聽香》
Thiann-Hiunn (Listening with Incense)

「聽香」是元宵節及中秋節的一項傳統習俗，即正月十五日或八月十五的夜晚，在神明前擲筊、問方向，依偷聽來的第一句話，預測這一年的運勢。

國立臺灣歷史博物館 藏
2004.019.0142

配天宮天上聖母籤詩雕版
Printing Plate of Mazu's Lottery
Poetry at Peitian Temple

臺灣的籤詩有 36 首、60 首、64 首、
100 首、120 首等，本件為朴子配天宮
運籤雕版，計 60 首。

國立臺灣歷史博物館　藏
2003.008.0762

天后宮藥籤拓本
Printed Medical Lots of the
Mazu Temple

在過去醫療不發達的時代，到廟宇求藥
籤，是民俗醫療的方法之一，藥籤內容
即是藥方，可分內科、外科、眼科、婦
人、小兒科等。本件為某天后宮藥籤拓
本 24 首（第 86-110 首，缺第 93 首）。

國立臺灣歷史博物館　藏／莊建緒捐贈
2010.003.0243

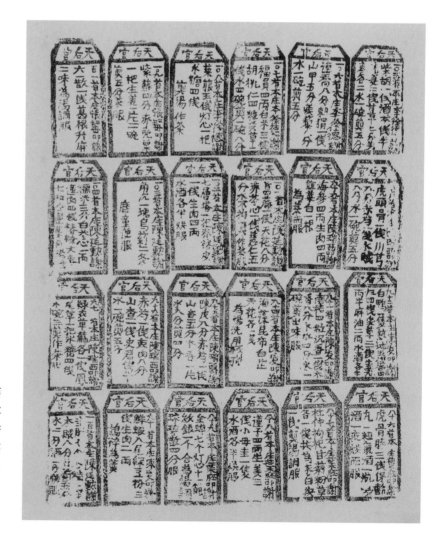

《推背圖》
The *Tuibeitu*

唐代袁天綱與李淳風所著《推背圖》，是中國三大預言書之一，共有60象，預測出中國從唐代武則天稱帝到清代滅亡的未來大事。後世有許多版本，本件為中央研究院藏本。

中央研究院歷史語言研究所傅斯年圖書館 藏

● 古今參考

試觀中國前賢劉伯溫纖譚清國隱語近今氣運是值二四一旗難蔽日思念遼陽舊家鄉東拜斗西拜旗南逐鹿北逐獅分南分北分東西此天數註定如孟子所謂順天者存逆天者亡可不慎歟試思二四一旗難蔽日思念遼陽舊家鄉此兩句既於光緒乙未丙申年經驗過了二四之數是八之數再加一數是九乙未丙申中年經驗過了八旗中國官入一旗合成九旗之號難蔽日之說是抵敵日本不駐難以遮蔽日逐陽之地是滿州人之舊家鄉因丙申年被日本官軍襲住而光緒君思念遼陽不甘心乃割台灣以易之並賠兵費而和約也現時正值東拜旗南逐鹿北逐獅此四句試靜思熟察古之米斗形體四方中加一斗梁北逐獅此形體似日字之形體現今日本之米斗亦然想此東拜斗之說必是向西方拜託日本也鹿身毛色有雜文合成一鹿想此西拜旗之說必是向東方拜託花旗逐鹿之說必是在中國南方驅逐雜處一鹿之名也美國之別名花旗才師二字北方有犬戎之名如數十小國湊之國想此北逐獅國北方驅逐犬戎之師旅也由此觀之可知數百年前之賢人能纖譚百年後之世事也天數註定非人所能改易也現時參觀清國新報紙所云維新黨首康有為李端棻徐致靖徐仁鑄徐仁鏡康廣仁宋伯魯楊深秀張蔭桓梁啟超於舊曆八月初旬本懃勤殿與光緒皇上議行新政立新營總統袁世凱調兵扼守舊黨迫害而袁世凱對日論明擥上論否則恐北洋大臣不聽其調遭兵退而袁世凱候旨卽論否則恐北洋大臣不聽其調遭兵退而袁世凱出恐事不諧急追袁同車趨出卽乘火車赴天津康有為上論令嗣同乘車追交袁世凱而袁世凱見袁世凱退祿榮祿立卽電奏皇太后袁世凱不奉詔以告直隸督榮而身佩其軍符及皇太后見宮監形色慌忙又身中鏜落洋銃一枝皇太后飭拿二閹人杖斃於八月初九日皇太后訓政飭拿維新黨交刑部訊斷正法謂光緒皇躬不豫令居瀛臺靜養休息各門戶添派二十名兵丁日夜往來嚴巡防守而康有為先逃往香港與英美人間答千言萬語皆是懇求英美兩國代維新黨報仇並保護光緒君等詞到九月初十日康有為又逃往日本神戶西拜旗日本長官派船出口外迎接入國由是觀之則東拜斗西拜旗其形跡顯然可見此天數之決定難移也而台灣眾民均是皆無或異自古以如祖父移於明朝民孫為清國民今為日本民即來錢糧租稅何代無之當知戒慎退自儆省乃無悔憾莫及之患也此存逆天者亡當知戒慎退自儆省乃無悔憾莫及之患也此管見議論之可否惟祈高明君子鑒察是非誠能各守本份各務本業無相劫奪無相貽害其享昇平豈不美哉

《臺灣日日新報》報導《燒餅歌》
News Report on the *Shaobing Song* on *Taiwan Daily News*

《燒餅歌》以易解的七言四句預言，廣為人知，也流通至臺灣。《臺灣日日新報》於明治31（1898）年11月20日刊載《燒餅歌》預測了臺灣割讓的天數，包括「二四一旗難蔽日，思念遼陽舊家鄉」二句喻意清朝甲午戰敗，臺灣割讓。及「東拜斗，西拜旗，南逐鹿，北逐獅，分南分北分東西」等句，則透露戊戌政變，康有為逃日，勸臺灣民眾順應天意，效忠日本。

來源：《臺灣日日新報》明治31（1898）年11月20日6版。漢珍數位圖書股份有限公司 提供。

命運女神涅墨西斯
Nemesis, or The Great Fortune

出生於紐倫堡、以版畫著名的德國藝術家阿爾布雷希特‧杜勒（Albrecht Dürer，1471-
1528），於 1501 年刻畫希臘神話的命運女神涅墨西斯（Nemesis）。版畫中的涅墨西斯，腳踏
球體保持平衡，是命運變幻不定的象徵。右手持獎盃，左手持鍊條，代表可能一手獎賞善行、一
手懲罰惡行，生動描繪出她是復仇女神，同時也是正義命運女神的形象。右下角有杜勒 AD 縮寫
簽名字樣。

科貝格聖經

Koberger-Bibel

德國紐倫堡重要印刷及出版商安東 · 科貝格（Anton Koberger）於 1483 年印製的德文聖經，也是馬丁路德劃時代翻譯《新約聖經》德文譯本之前的第 9 版德文聖經。聖經中記載了先知的啟示與預言，成了基督徒最熟悉的預言故事，其中《啟示錄》更預言了世界末日，描繪出現十角七頭獸的異象，被視為魔鬼、敵基督、世俗力量等象徵。

日耳曼國家博物館　藏
Germanisches Nationalmuseum, Nuremberg, Germany

約翰吃小書卷
Saint John Devouring the Book

德國藝術家阿爾布雷希特 · 杜勒（Albrecht Dürer）木刻版畫，出自聖經書頁，描繪《啟示錄》第 10 章中，身披雲彩、腳像火柱的大天使從天降臨，手中拿著展開的書卷，指示使徒約翰，取走書卷並吃盡它，便腹苦口蜜，要約翰領略書的內容（神道），再說預言的故事。

日耳曼國家博物館 Collection Bernhard Hausmann 藏
Germanisches Nationalmuseum, Nuremberg, Germany. Collection Bernhard Hausmann.

Von der dritten Sibylla.

Sibylla Delphica/ein sunderlich fürnemige Weissage-
rin/Ist zü ihren zeiten/als Eusebius schreibt/in grossen
Ehren gewesen. Chrisippus schreibt auch von ihr/im büch von der
Gotheit. Würt Delphica gnañt/von der stat Delphi/da sie im
Tempel Apollinis geboren ist/Schwartz bekleydt/hat ein horn
in ihrer hand. Hat mercklich vom Troianischen krieg/Von der
geburt/leben vñ sterben Christi/geweissagt/under andern also.

Du solt erkennen deinen eygnen Herren/der ein warer Got-
tes Sün ist. Vnd an einem andern ende. Es würdt geboren
ein Prophet/on leiblich vermischung der müter/auß seiner jung
frawen ꝛc. Das sagt auch die Geschrifft einhelliglich/als. Got
würdt euch erwecken einen Propheten auß euweren brüderen/
den werdent ihr hören als mich/on leibliche vermischung der mü-
ter. Off das sagt das Euangelium. Ich hab keynen man
erkandt/Also hat Maria dem Ertzengel Gabriel geantwortet.
Dañ das in ihr geboren/das ist von dem heiligen Geyst/Dañ er
nit von menlichem samen kommen ist.

Dauon sagt auch der Prophet Isaias. Nim war ein Jung
fraw würdt empfahen/vnd würdt geberen einen Sün.

Hieremias am Dreiundzweintzigsten
Capitel.

Sehent die Tage kommen/spricht der Herr/Vnd ich werde
erquicken Dauid die gerechte blüm/vnd der Küng würdt Re-
gieren vnd würdt weise/vnd thüt das Vrtheil vnd die gerechtig
keit im land/Zü seiner zeit würdt Juda geholffen/vnd Israel
würdt sicher wonen.

B iij

《12 位女先知預言》
Twelve Sibylline Oracles

西比拉（sibyl）是指古希臘的神諭者、女先知，她們與神溝
通、領受神諭，並預言未來，其預言在歐洲中世紀時期深受
重視。本書由 16 世紀德國法蘭克福著名印刷及出版商克里
斯蒂安 ・ 埃格諾夫（Christian Egenolff）於 1531 年以德
文出版，收錄了 12 位女先知的預言，包括為人熟知的德爾
菲女先知（Sibylla Delphica）。

日耳曼國家博物館 藏
Germanisches Nationalmuseum, Nuremberg, Germany

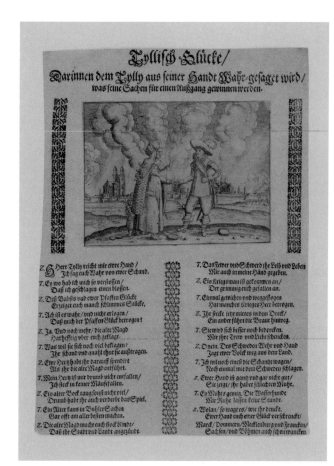

典型的命運傳單
Leaflet: "Tilly's Fortune"

1631 年馬格德堡戰役（Sack of Magdeburg）是三十
年戰爭死傷最嚴重的一場戰役，本件 1631 年的傳單是
描述帶領天主教聯軍的約翰‧塞爾克拉斯‧提利伯爵
（Johann Cerklas von Tilly）圍攻新教城市馬格德堡，
找一位占卜師諮詢、看手相，占卜師預言將有一個嚴峻
的未來。

日耳曼國家博物館 藏
Germanisches Nationalmuseum, Nuremberg, Germany

1632 年先知預言傳單
Leaflet: "Prophetic Prophecy"

三十年戰爭，發生於 1618-1648 年間，是一場由宗教改
革引發的歐洲大戰，也是日耳曼民族重大的歷史創傷。
本件 1632 年的傳單描述帶領天主教聯軍的約翰‧塞爾
克拉斯‧提利爵（Johann Cerklas von Tilly）於 1632
年 4 月雨之戰（Battle of Rain）的失敗，被視為聖經預
言的實現。

日耳曼國家博物館 藏
Germanisches Nationalmuseum, Nuremberg, Germany

《梵蒂岡教宗預言》
Papal Prophecies- Vaticinia de summis pontificibus

《梵蒂岡教宗預言》出版於 1464-1471 年間，最初被認為與紅衣主教有關，後來被確認為教宗的繼承，常見以小冊子流通。內容為 30 條未來教宗的預言，從 13 世紀尼閣三世（Nicholas III）、到 15 世紀西方大分裂教宗退位、敵基督的出現結束。預言可能出自於 9 世紀後期拜占庭的「利奧神諭」（Leo Oracles），經 11 或 12 世紀的更新，13 世紀幾次不同版本的結合，由 16 條確立為 30 條。

日耳曼國家博物館 藏
Germanisches Nationalmuseum, Nuremberg, Germany

席 · 傑勒吉藍繪《飛魚之神託夢》
The Flying Fish Spirit Coming to Dreams

《飛魚之神託夢》描繪飛魚神向雅美族長老告知有關食用飛魚的方法與相關禁忌的夢境情景，這就是雅美族飛魚祭的由來。

國立臺灣歷史博物館 藏
2005.005.0069

《狀元圖考》
Zhuang Yuan Tu Kao

不同的文化會產生不同類型的夢，本件為明代顧祖訓編撰的夢書，記載了明代狀元各種的「狀元夢」，呈現科舉制度下讀書人的占夢文化。

國家圖書館 藏

《周公解夢》
The Duke of Zhou's Explanation of Dreams

依夢的主題，分為 27 類，是民間廣為流傳的解夢書。

竹林書局 發行

約瑟為法老解夢
Joseph Interpreting the Pharaoh's Dream

有能力解釋夢境的人，自古以來享有非凡的權威與智慧。本件原件為製作於 1540-1550 年間的彩繪玻璃畫，描繪聖經《創世紀》約瑟為埃及法老王解釋「七頭牛與七穗麥子」夢境的含意，預測出埃及七年豐年之後將有七年荒年，畫中人物穿著當時 16 世紀的衣服。

日耳曼國家博物館 藏
Germanisches Nationalmuseum, Nuremberg, Germany

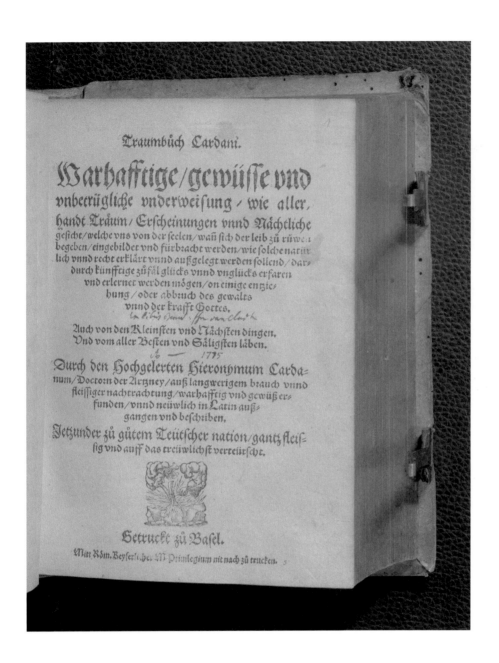

《夢書》
Traumbuch Cardani

歐洲自古典時代以來，流傳著許多解夢的著作。由義大利占星家、數學家、醫師的吉羅拉莫・卡爾達諾（Geronimo Cardano，1501-1576）撰寫的《夢書》（Somniorum synesiorum omnis generis insomnia explicantes, Libri IIII），將夢境進行理論分析，包括夢的原因、夢的分類、建議如何解讀等，翻譯成許多不同語言版本，成為家喻戶曉解夢的參考書，本件為 1563 年出版德文譯本。

日耳曼國家博物館 藏
Germanisches Nationalmuseum, Nuremberg, Germany

扶乩與通靈

Fuji and Spirit Mediums

Automatisches Schreiben und Mediumismus

乩童、鸞生、尪姨、巫師、靈媒⋯⋯等，因能與神靈溝通，往往被視為掌握神秘知識與擁有魔法的人，通靈因而成為預測未來的方法之一。臺灣的扶鸞，是一種降神的方式，由讀書人的鸞生執行，透過桃木與柳枝組成的鸞筆，在神明降靈時，於沙盤上寫下神示的旨意（鸞文）。有些會再由鸞生將之集結成書，藉以勸善。自清以來，許多儒生、地方仕紳參與扶乩。在臺灣歷史上，1915 年的西來庵事件就與鸞堂有關。

Tongji, luansheng, shamans, and other spirit mediums are believed to have knowledge of the occult and possess supernatural powers to communicate with deities, making mediumship a way to predict the future. The *fuluan* (spirit writing) in Taiwan is a form of séance carried out by *luansheng* (spirit writers) who write divine texts in sand with a spirit brush made of peach wood and a willow branch. Some *luansheng* also compile divinations into books for moral education. As *fuluan* requires reading and writing, it is customary for scholars and the local gentry to be involved in the practice of *fuluan*. In the history of Taiwan, the Tapani Incident in 1915 was related to the use of *fuluan*.

帶卜辭龜腹甲《丙》0469
Inscribed Tortoise Plastron

甲骨占卜的過程，是占卜前先在龜甲或獸骨的背面進行鑽鑿，占卜時再於鑽鑿處灼燒，正面就會裂出「卜」形的卜兆，根據卜兆判斷吉凶，最後再把卜辭刻寫上去。本件是為了求雨而舉行祭祀的占卜。其中「𤈦」是焚殘疾人以祭祀求雨。「𣥏」是跳舞求雨。

中央研究院歷史語言研究所 藏

帶填硃卜辭獸骨殘片
Inscribed Bovid Scapula

本件甲骨為肩胛骨的上部，正面卜問狩獵是否有收穫，背面的驗辭紀錄商王獵得九隻豬。

中央研究院歷史語言研究所 藏

掃描 QR Code
可觀看 3D 模型

排灣族巫具箱
A Paiwan Shamanistic Toolbox

排灣族每位女巫師都有自己的
巫具箱，是巫師身分的代表，
做祭儀時巫師通常隨身佩戴。
巫具箱由木箱及網袋組成，通
常放有青銅刀、豬骨、榕樹葉、
神珠（無患子果實）等物。

國立臺灣博物館 藏

阿美族祭壺
An Amis Ritualistic Pot

採集自花蓮縣吉安鄉的阿
美族祭壺，質地粗厚，推
測為雄性祭壺 (dewas)，
通常裝酒，與男性的狩獵
與祭祀有關。

國立臺灣博物館 藏

泰雅族竹占用具
Atayal Bamboo Divination Tools

依收藏來源指本件為泰雅族南澳群使用之
竹占用具。占卜時，巫師蹲下以膝蓋夾住
細竹管，然後將圓珠（穿孔玻璃珠）放置
於竹管上，一面唸咒，如果圓珠沒有掉落，
代表「是」，若掉下來，代表「否」。

秋惠文庫林于昉 提供

泰雅族占卜用具
Atayal Divination Tools

泰雅族溪頭群使用的占卜用具，包括占卜玻璃
罐、植物根莖罐蓋、三角形竹片及方形小竹片，
皆以麻繩串縛。

國立臺灣博物館 藏

鸞筆
Phoenix Brush

鸞筆是扶鸞儀式重要的用具，由 V 型分枝的桃木接上柳枝組合而成，象徵陰陽調和。儀式舉行時，由單人或雙人鸞生手持操作，於沙盤或桌面上寫下神諭。本件頭部刻有龍頭紋。

國立臺灣歷史博物館 藏
2018.024.0232

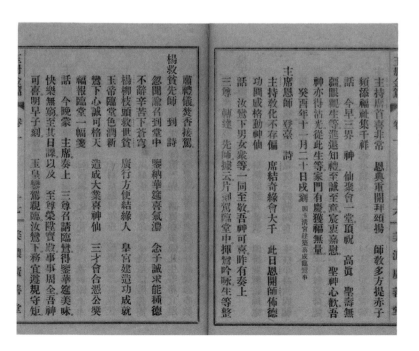

美濃廣善堂出版《玉冊金篇》
Yu-ce-jin-pian

早期的鸞堂大都由仕紳、儒生所主持，集結鸞文出版的「鸞書」或「善書」，也多以儒家倫理為主，勸人為善。本件為創立於 1917 年的美濃廣善堂，於昭和 11（1936）年出版之鸞書。

國立臺灣歷史博物館 藏
2006.006.0860

手輦
Divination Chair

多使用於降乩，供信徒問事儀式。

―――――――――

國立臺灣歷史博物館 藏／黃素珍捐贈
2004.054.0001

黃金田繪《扶手輦》
The Divination Chair

描繪鄉人們至廟宇問事、桌頭「辦事」
的情景。

―――――――――

國立臺灣歷史博物館 藏
2004.019.0062

刺球、月斧、銅棍、七星劍、鯊魚劍
A Taoist Spiky Ball, a Taoist Crescent Axe, a Taoist Mace, a Taoist Seven Star Sword, and a Taoist Shark Sword

刺球、月斧、銅棍、七星劍、鯊魚劍（由左至右），是乩童降乩或降駕時 5 件重要的法器，又稱為「乩童五寶」。降乩時會以五寶砍劈頭部或背部，透過見血來召請五營兵將或辟邪，也會配合五營之方位進行操五寶。

國立臺灣歷史博物館 藏
2003.001.0398、2019.013.0083
2010.031.0320、2010.031.0305、2003.001.0924

黃金田繪《乩童起駕敕符道》
Tongji in Séance

國立臺灣歷史博物館 藏
2004.019.0064

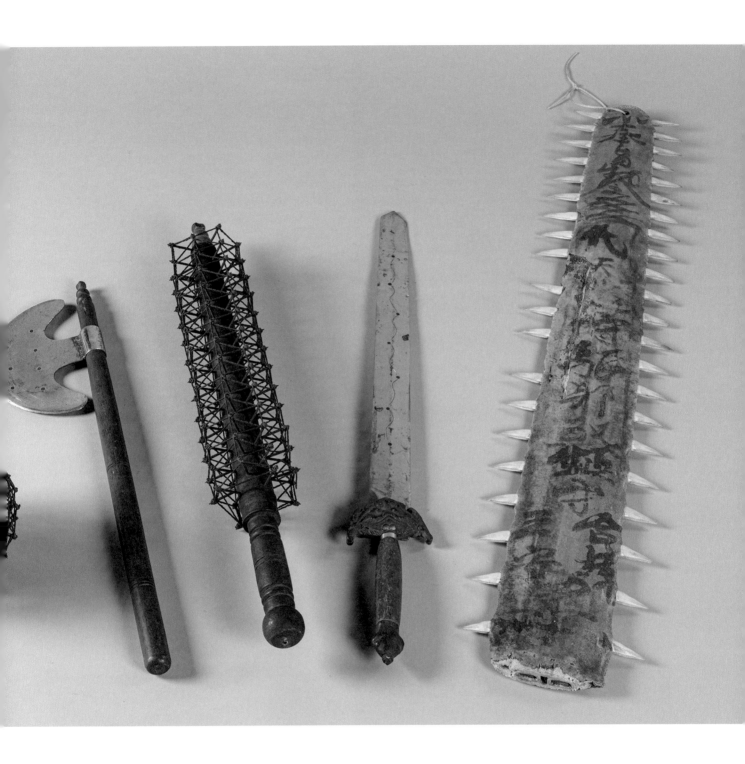

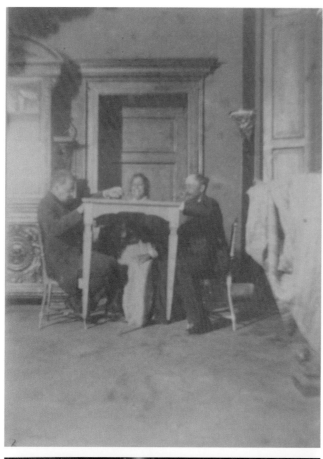

旋桌術
Table-Tipping

旋桌術於 19 世紀中期從美國傳入歐洲。歐莎皮亞・帕拉迪諾（Eusapia Palladino，1854-1918）是義大利著名的靈媒，她聲稱具有可以讓桌子懸浮、移動物體等超自然能力，吸引了歐洲科學家們的注意，本件是她於1892年在米蘭舉辦降神會、操作旋桌術的情景，參與者包括藝術家、醫生等。

日耳曼國家博物館 藏
Germanisches Nationalmuseum, Nuremberg, Germany

水晶球
Crystal Ball

歐洲的占卜術，水晶被視為可與惡魔、天使等交流、獲取信息的用具，19 世紀隨著相信靈魂永恆不死的唯靈論出現後，人們相信可以透過水晶球與靈魂溝通。本件為 19 世紀中期製作的水晶球。

日耳曼國家博物館 藏
Germanisches Nationalmuseum, Nuremberg, Germany

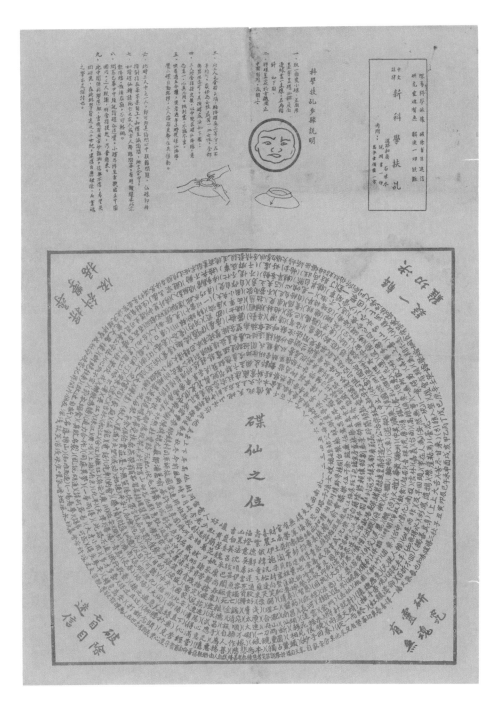

碟仙
Ouija Board

曾在臺灣風行一時的碟仙，號稱「新科學扶乩」，占卜方式與歐美的通靈板、旋桌術等類似。操作時大家圍坐碟子旁，一起將食指按定於碟子邊緣，默求碟仙降臨，問出心中的問題，再讓碟子指出於某字句上，即為碟仙的解答。

國立臺灣歷史博物館 藏／洪輝龍捐贈
2009.007.0009

04 扭轉運勢

Changing One's Destiny
Umkehr der Vorsehung

人們透過占卜獲得了關於命運跟未來的預測結果後，為了趨吉避凶，在歐洲與臺灣有一些共通的做法。例如配戴或是擺設護身符、避邪物或幸運物。臺灣漢人社會受到道教影響，常見的有平安符、治病符、鎮宅符等，同時也有劍獅、山海鎮、風獅爺、石敢當等厭勝的器物。歐洲則有以動物、植物、寶石製作護身符。此外，為了破解厄運，臺灣還有透過法師、或道士進行「祭解」（又稱補運、改運）儀式，為流年不順或家運不濟的人解除關煞，常見者有以紙人作為替身，代替本人而承受厄運，或以白虎紙錢、天狗紙錢、五鬼紙錢等祭煞錢來消災解厄。

✖

Having divined one's destiny and future, there are steps that people can take to change or ensure that they happen. The wearing or placement of amulets, talismans, or lucky charms, for example, are common in both Europe and Taiwan. With a prevalent belief in Taoism, the most common wearable amulets in Han Taiwanese society are peace amulets *(pinganfu)*, healing amulets *(zhibingfu)*, and house-guarding amulets *(zhengzhaifu)*, and the talismans include sword lions, *shanhaizhen* (an image with a eight-hexagram pattern and scenes of mountains and the sea), wind lion god statues, and *shigandang* (a stone tablet with writing). In Europe, amulets might be made of animals, plants, or jewelry. In addition, to fend off misfortune, there are Taoist masters in Taiwan who can perform amelioration rituals *(jijie)* or "supply" good fortune for people suffering adversities. Such rituals are usually performed using a paper figure as the "stand-in" of oneself to take the misfortune or by offering the paper "malefic money" of *baihu* (white tiger), *tiengo* (dog of heaven), and *wugui* (five ghosts) to buy one's way out of misfortune and disaster.

Nachdem Menschen durch Wahrsagen eine Vorhersage über ihr Schicksal und ihre Zukunft erhalten haben, gibt es in Europa sowie in Taiwan einige übereinstimmende Methoden, um das Glück zu suchen und das Unglück zu vermeiden. So kann man etwa ein Schutzamulett, ein Apotropaion oder einen Glücksbringer tragen. Die ethnische Han in Taiwan ist stark vom Daoismus beeinflusst, so gibt es etwa Talismane zur Schutzamulett, zur Heilung von Krankheiten und dem Schutz der Wohnstätte. Außerdem gibt es Schwertlöwen, Berg-Meer-Siegel, Wächterlöwen, Bannfels und viele weitere das Unglück abwehrende Objekte. In Europa hingegen gibt es Schutzamulette, die aus Tieren, Pflanzen und Edelsteinen hergestellt werden. Hiervon abgesehen gibt es in Taiwan zur Abwendung eines bösen Schicksals noch die Möglichkeit, durch einen Priester der Volksreligion oder des Daoismus eine Zeremonie zur Änderung des Schicksals durchführen zu lassen. Um für Menschen, die schlechte Jahre erleben oder bei denen das Familienglück brüchig ist die vorherbestimmten Probleme in ihrem Schicksal aufzuheben, nutzen diese häufig Papiermännchen als Stellvertreter, die an Stelle der Geschädigten das Unglück auf sich nehmen. Außerdem nutzen sie oft Weißer-Tiger-Papiergeld, Himmelshund-Papiergeld, Fünf-Geister-Papiergeld und andere Sorten rituellen Papiergeldes, um das Unglück zu beseitigen.

扭轉運勢

人們透過占卜獲得了關於命運跟未來的預測結果後，為了趨吉避凶，在歐洲與臺灣有一些共通的做法。例如配戴或是擺設護身符、避邪物或幸運物。臺灣漢人社會受到道教影響，常見的有平安符、治病符、鎮宅符等，同時也有劍獅、山海鎮、風獅爺、石敢當等厭勝的器物。歐洲則有以動物、植物、寶石製作護身符。此外，為了破解厄運，臺灣還有透過法師，或道士進行「祭解」（又稱補運、改運）儀式，為流年不順或家運不濟的人解除關煞，常見者有以紙人作為替身，代替本人而承受厄運，或以白虎紙錢、天狗紙錢、五鬼紙錢等祭煞紙錢來消災解厄。

Changing One's Destiny

Having divined one's destiny and future, there are steps that people can take to change or amend that step, bumps. The wearing or placement of amulets, talismans, or lucky charms, for example, are common in both Europe and Taiwan. With a prevalent belief in Taoism, the more common protective amulets in Han Taiwanese society are peace amulets (ping-an fu), healing amulets (zhi-bing fu), and house-guarding amulets (zhen-zhai fu) and the talismanic animals sword lions, shan-hai zhen (an image with a Bagua pattern and scenes of mountains and the sea), wind lion god statues, and objects to ward off evil spirits. In Europe, amulets might be made of animals, plants, or jewelry. In addition, to ward off misfortune, there are Taoist masters in Taiwan who perform exorcism rituals (jijie) or "supply" good fortune for people suffering adversities. Said rituals are usually performed using a paper figure as the "stand-in" of oneself to take the misfortune or by offering the paper "mystic money" of Baihu (white tiger), Tiangu (dog of heaven) and Wugui (five ghosts) to buy one's way out of misfortune and disaster.

Umkehr der Vorsehung

Nachdem Menschen durch Wahrsagen das Schicksal oder die Zukunft mit ihrer Vorausschau erahnen konnten, gibt es in Europa und in Taiwan einige gemeinsame Methoden um das Gute zu suchen und das Böse zu meiden. So können etwa das Tragen oder das Aufstellen von Amuletten, um Unglück oder magie, die abwehren Böse in Taiwan oder sich Glücksbringer ausüben. Die Han-taiwanische Gesellschaft wurde durch den Taoismus beeinflusst, üblich sind hier Friedenstalismane, Heiltalismane, Hausschutztalismane und auch Gegenstände wie Schwert-Löwen, Berg-Meer-Bilder, Windlöwen-Gottstatuen und Steinwächter. In Europa bestehen sie z.B. aus Tieren, Pflanzen und wertvollen Juwelen als Talismane. Außerdem, gibt es in Taiwan um exorzistischen von Taoist-Priestern durch Leuten, den Unglück von Schicksals oder Jahreslauf zu lösen, wird ein Person aus Schicksalsträger als das Leidende oder mittels der des geheimnisvollen Papiergeldern Weise Baihu (weißer Tiger) Tiangu (Himmelshund) oder Wugui (fünf Geister) zur Geldmittel. So können der Unglück und Katastrophen heraus kaufen.

天師鎮宅版印符令
**Talisman of Celestial Master
Chang for Peaceful Home**

天師鎮宅符，具有鎮宅平安之功能。

國立臺灣歷史博物館 藏
2003.008.0693

黑緞地彩繡龜鹿香袋
**Turtle and Deer Sachet with
Embroidery on Black Silk**

民間傳說端午節配戴香包，可以辟
邪消災。本件一面繡有口銜竹葉的
鹿，另一面繡有烏龜，象徵「得祿、
長壽」，從刺繡技法和圖樣推測為
苗栗客家地區的傳統繡品。

國立臺灣歷史博物館 藏
2003.008.0408

**南鯤鯓代天府五府千歲
版印平安符**
A Printed Five *Wangye* Safety
Talisman of the Nankunshen
Temple

臺南北門的南鯤鯓代天府，主祀五
府千歲，素有「王爺總廟」之譽。
其平安符，為臺灣常見的平安符型
式。

國立臺灣歷史博物館 藏
2003.008.0644

天王宮護身保命版印平安符
A Printed Safety Talisman
of the Tienwang Temple

國立臺灣歷史博物館 藏
2003.008.0646

三奶夫人斬煞治病符
The Three Ladies Malefic
Slaying and Healing Talisman

三奶夫人指的是陳靖姑、林九娘、
李三娘等三位夫人神，以陳靖姑為
首，為福建地區的地方神明。民間
習俗相信三奶夫人的符令，具有斬
煞治病之法力。

國立臺灣歷史博物館 藏／莊建緒捐贈
2010.003.0173

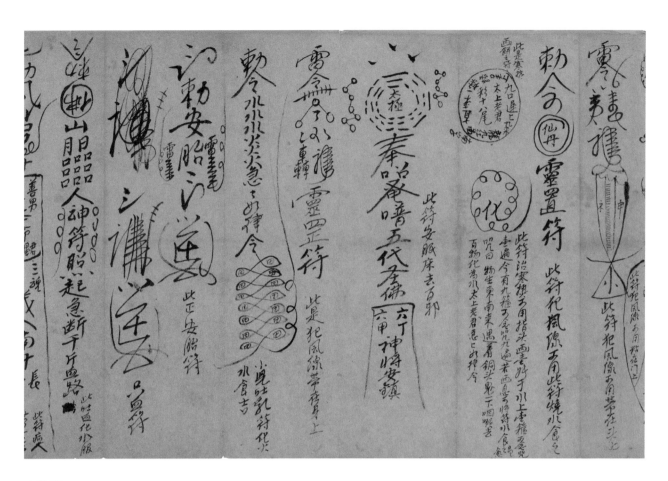

安胎符
A Tocolysis Talisman

婦女懷孕生產的過程,影響著孕婦與胎兒的生命安全,風險極高。民間習俗相信胎兒是受胎神支配的,如果沖犯胎神就會生病,因此為求生產順利,常會請道長進行安胎儀式,將安胎符貼在床柱或房門口,或燒化符令喝下,可保孕婦及胎兒平安。本件為「符仔師」手抄各種符令的符仔簿,此頁的安胎符是常見的型式。

國立臺灣歷史博物館 藏
2003.007.0108

鷹石護身符
Eagle-Stone with Wire and Eyelet

製作於 16-17 世紀的鷹石護身符。鷹石是一種空心的岩石,內部含有晶體或小石頭等,搖晃時會發出嘎嘎聲,人們認為這種「懷孕的石頭」,會生出其他石頭,因而在歐洲及中東地區作為護身符,幫助婦女生產。綁在孕婦手臂上,保護胎兒、防止流產;綁在大腿上,助於順利生產

日耳曼國家博物館 藏
Germanisches Nationalmuseum, Nuremberg, Germany

牛黃
Bezoar

牛黃即動物的胃腸道結石，具有全面的治療功效，可以解毒、解熱、抗痛風、癲癇，治療胃痛、噁心、暈眩、腹瀉等症狀。歐洲除當藥材使用外，可以作為護身符，裝在小袋子隨身佩戴，保護佩戴者 24 小時內不受任何影響。鍍金的牛黃，被視為具有防止風暴的保護效果。

日耳曼國家博物館 藏
Germanisches Nationalmuseum, Nuremberg, Germany

疾病護身符
Talisman Made from
Seven Metals

製作於 16-18 世紀，歐洲使用的硬幣形式護身符，由煉金術士以金、銀、銅、鐵、汞、錫、鉛等 7 種金屬材質合成製作，據說作為項鍊隨身佩戴、或放在枕頭下，可以防止痛風、癲癇、風濕病、皮疹等疾病發作。正面以太陽為中心，周圍環繞 7 種金屬對應 7 大行星符號，即金—太陽（☉），銀—月亮（☽），銅—金星（♀），鐵—火星（♂），汞—水星（☿），錫—木星（♃），鉛—土星（♄）。背面為虛構的紋樣，最外圈銘文說明功效。

日耳曼國家博物館 藏
Germanisches Nationalmuseum,
Nuremberg, Germany

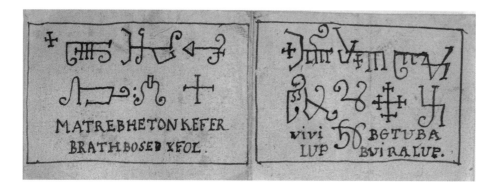

帶有符咒的護身符
Amulet Cards with
Magical Characters and
Words

16、17 世紀的符咒護身符，上印有祈禱文字、或咒語、與神奇符號。其魔法符號可能代表行星和自然元素，還包括天使、惡魔和其他超自然力量。使用上通常是綁在或縫在衣服上、或食用。

日耳曼國家博物館 藏
Germanisches Nationalmuseum,
Nuremberg, Germany

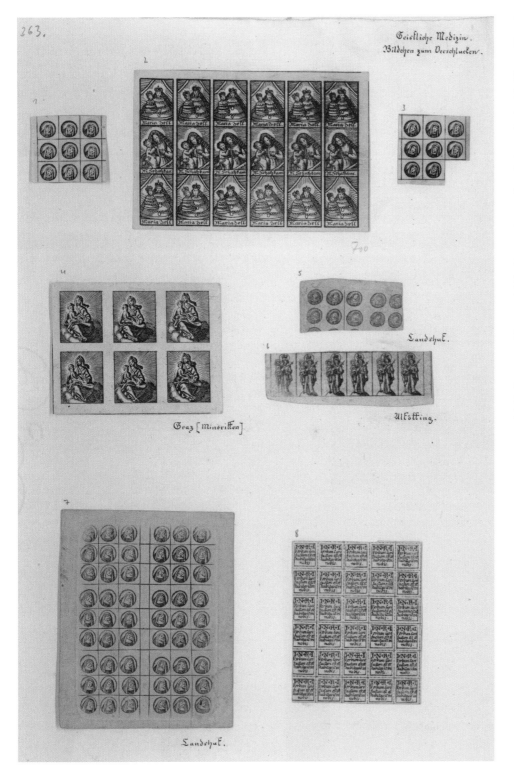

可食用的護身符
Schluckbildchen

郵票大小、印著聖母瑪麗亞、或聖母與聖子肖像圖的護身符，可在許多朝聖地購買，例如德國阿爾特廷（Altötting）與奧地利瑪麗亞采爾（Mariazell）等，提供給朝聖者，餵給生病的孩子或牛隻吃、或放在身上，獲得治療功效。這是在天主教允許下的魔法替代品，也是18-20世紀被視為民俗醫療的方式。

日耳曼國家博物館 藏
Germanisches
Nationalmuseum,
Nuremberg, Germany

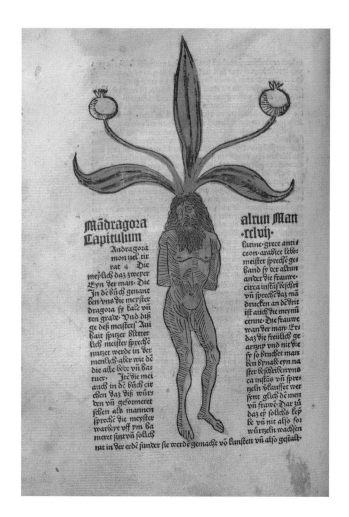

魔法藥草曼陀羅
Mandrake

曼陀羅是西方文化史著名的魔法植物,主要在於它的根部類似人形,屬稀有且昂貴的藥草。在歐洲早期藥草書中,將其擬人化,強化其魔力。例如自然史作家約翰內斯 · 德 · 古巴(Johannes de Cuba)於1485年出版的藥草書《Gart der Gesundheit》,是最早以德文印刷的藥草書之一,將曼陀羅描繪成男性及女性的身形。

日耳曼國家博物館 藏
Germanisches Nationalmuseum, Nuremberg, Germany

桃梗
Taogeng Talisman

根據考證,這些面貌兇惡的木人,很可能是漢代人用來避惡鬼和凶邪的桃符。木人下端尖銳,以便插在門戶上。

中央研究院歷史語言研究所 藏

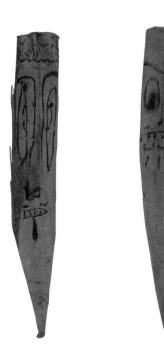

風獅爺
Wind Lion God Statue

風獅爺，一般立於屋頂，是民宅和村落常設
的厭勝物，具有鎮風、壓煞、驅邪的功能。

國立臺灣歷史博物館 藏／李啟繁捐贈
2002.008.0208

八卦劍獅牌
Eight Trigram Lion with Double Swords Charm

八卦劍獅牌，結合了劍獅與八卦，是常見的辟邪物之一，
主要懸掛於窗戶或門楣上方，用以鎮制宅沖、柱沖等煞氣。
本件使用常見的辟邪顏色—綠色，造型上做雙眼圓錚、唧
咬七星劍、上額有八卦，是臺灣早期常見的劍獅獸牌型式。

國立臺灣歷史博物館 藏
2003.019.0064

山海鎮
Shanhaizhen

山海鎮是臺灣常見的辟邪物之一，通常懸掛在
民宅正門上方，常見者畫有山、海、日、月、
八卦等圖案，並於二側寫有「我家如山海」、「他
作我無妨」等字，藉由山海的力量，鎮煞、辟邪。

國立臺灣歷史博物館 藏
2002.001.0020

安奉太歲符
The *Taisui* Pacifying Talisman

本件安奉太歲符為印記拓印，原符使用時多用
紅紙墨版印製。民間習俗相信生肖流年遇有坐
太歲、沖太歲時，需安奉值年太歲星君，祈守
護元辰、化解災厄，多於農曆新年期間安奉，
並在歲末送神時謝退。

國立臺灣歷史博物館 藏／莊建緒捐贈
2010.003.0195

八卦五雷符
The *Bagua* and Five-Thunders Talisman

五雷為道教主要的自然信仰，擁有強大之法力
而能斬邪除祟，常見以五雷令牌召五雷以辟邪。
五雷符，則具有收斬邪鬼、滅邪的功能，加上
八卦、日月之形，更增靈力。

國立臺灣歷史博物館 藏
2006.007.0018

追魂馬版畫
Soul-Capturing Horse Print

追魂馬紙錢為特殊紙錢，主要用於祭解、補運儀式。臺灣民間
習俗相信人在運勢欠佳時，會有散失魂魄的情形，容易導致精
神不佳、疾病纏身，必須進行祭解補運加以改善，燒化追魂馬
紙錢，即能追回散失之魂魄。

國立臺灣歷史博物館 藏
2004.025.1059

藏魂罐組
Soul-Concealing Jar Set

藏魂又稱蓋魂、嵌魂，藏魂改運法為民間常見的改運法術之
一。當一個人流年運勢欠佳或沖犯神煞時，可以將頭髮、指甲
及生辰八字放入罐中，以紅布、符令蓋封，就可以將自己的壞
運蓋起來。

國立臺灣歷史博物館 藏
2006.003.0179

道士袍
A Daoist Master Robe

臺灣的道士,可分為專辦吉事的「紅頭道士」,與兼辦吉事與喪事的「烏頭道
士」。烏頭道士,通常頭戴黑色網巾與金色道冠,儀式時穿著道士袍,是廟會
建醮、祭解、補運等類吉事的靈魂人物。本件有袖正面開襟的道士袍,繡有團
鶴紋,是嘉義以南至屏東、澎湖等地區道士常穿的式樣。

國立臺灣歷史博物館 藏
2005.006.0467

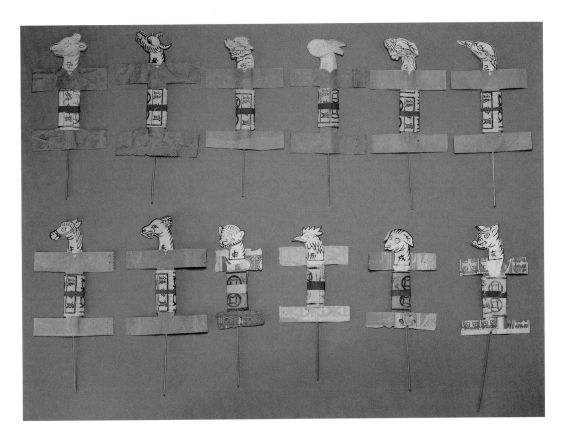

十二生肖替身組
Stand-in Figures of the 12 Chinese Zodiac Signs

替身為祭解法術用以代替本人承受厄運的用品，本組為十二生肖替身，分為子鼠、丑牛、寅虎、卯兔、辰龍、巳蛇、午馬、未羊、申猴、酉雞、戌狗、亥豬等合十二地支年份所生之人，以買命錢包裹身軀。

國立臺灣歷史博物館　藏
2003.008.0542

男女替身紙像
Male and Female Stand-In Paper Figure

製作於宜蘭地區。

國立臺灣歷史博物館　藏／莊建緒捐贈
2010.003.0136、2010.003.0141

本命錢紙錢
The Natal-Year Paper Money

本命錢又稱「陰陽本命錢」，一般配合改連真經、
替身使用，用於改運。民間習俗相信若逢年度沖
煞太歲、天狗、白虎、五鬼等神煞，或犯惡疾、
車關、血光等災厄時，可至壇廟中進行祭解，祭
以小三牲等，並以本命錢、改連經等加強陰陽本
命，達到補運、改運之功能。

國立臺灣歷史博物館 藏
2003.008.0623

白虎紙錢
The White-Tiger Paper Money

白虎紙錢用以禳祭白虎煞。白虎與太歲、五鬼、
天狗等常見的關煞神，民間習俗認為流年生肖犯
白虎，易有血光災病外傷等厄運，必須進行祭解
儀式，以解厄運。

國立臺灣歷史博物館 藏／莊建緒捐贈
2003.024.0088

改連真經陰陽本命錢連幅紙錢
**Fortune-Amelioration Mantra with Natal-Year
Yin Yang Paper Money**

改連真經又稱為「改年真經」，一般多與本命錢、男女
替身合用，是改運補運專用的紙錢。本件來自宜蘭羅東
正義紙莊，為當代常見的橫幅型式。

國立臺灣歷史博物館 藏／莊建緒捐贈
2010.003.0124

天狗紙錢
The Heavenly-Dog Paper Money

天狗煞為常見的流年煞神，主口舌、損傷、多勞煩心之厄。若流年地支沖犯天狗，易遭小人陷害，須禳祭以辟厄。

———————————

國立臺灣歷史博物館 藏／莊建緒捐贈
2010.003.0075

五鬼紙錢
The Five-Ghosts Paper Money

五鬼即五行之煞。若流年地支沖犯五鬼，易有破耗、官司等厄難，須祭五鬼以避不好的事發生。

———————————

國立臺灣歷史博物館 藏
2003.008.0622

買命錢紙錢
Paper Money for Buying Life

買命錢，主要用於制化短命關、取命關等關煞，亦可在生命危急時使用。本件來自宜蘭頭城茂惠紙店（茂惠金香鋪）。

———————————

國立臺灣歷史博物館 藏
2010.003.0038

煞神紙錢
Paper Money for the Malefic Deities

臺灣民間相信若遇有不明災難，多為各種煞神所致，必須祭拜，方可保平安。煞神紙錢即用以祭祀煞神，獻紙錢於煞神，即可脫離厄運。

———————————

國立臺灣歷史博物館 藏
2003.008.0619

05

占卜的人們

Fortune-Telling and -Hearing
Die Menschen, welche wahrsagen

常言道：「歹命人愛算命」、「算命嘴，胡累累」、「算命沒褒，吃水都沒」，一語道破問事者與占卜者的刻板印象。占卜者掌握了代言神諭或解讀詮釋各種徵兆以滿足問事者的需求。但不論在歐洲或臺灣，他們一般社會地位不高，也常受教會、政府、知識份子的批評；雖然這些團體中的人也常尋求占者的意見。日本時代的張麗俊、林獻堂、吳新榮等臺灣知識份子，對占卜見解不同，但占卜仍深植他們和各階層人們的日常生活中。即便今日，臺灣大部分人都曾有過安太歲、算命或取名字的經驗，顯見人們對占測命運的興趣，歷久不衰。

✕

Sayings in Taiwan such as "it's always the misfortunate ones who need fortune-telling," "a fortune-teller has a mouth of gibberish," or "fortune-tellers make a living through flattery" reveal stereotypes of fortune-tellers and those who seek their advice. Although fortune-tellers interpret oracles and omens and provide suggestions to whoever might need their opinions, they possess a lower social status and are often criticized by disparate religious institutions, ruling groups, or intellectuals, both in Europe and Taiwan. Despite this, many critics have still sought opinions from fortune-tellers. During the Japanese era, both commoners and intellectuals in Taiwan, such as Li-jun Chang, Hsien-tang Lin, and Hsin-jung Wu, all embraced fortune telling, their divergent views on divination notwithstanding. Most people in Taiwan have had some kind of experience related to fortune telling, such as pacifying *taisui (antaisui)*, seeking out fortune tellers, or choosing a name, demonstrating how the desire to know and predict one's future has both been sustained and evolved over time.

In Taiwan gibt es diese Sprichwörter: „Leute mit schlechtem Schicksal lieben es, sich wahrsagen zu lassen ", „Wahrsager reden sich selbst müde " und „Wenn ein Wahrsager keine Komplimente macht, hat er nicht einmal Wasser zum Trinken ". Damit werden die Klischees über den Fragenden und den Wahrsager auf den Punkt gebracht. Der Wahrsager hat die Macht, als Orakel für die Gottheit zu sprechen oder verschiedene Zeichen so zu deuten, dass sie den Bedürfnissen des Fragenden entsprechen. Dennoch ist ihr gesellschaftlicher Status sowohl in Europa als auch in Taiwan normalerweise nicht hoch, und sie werden oft von Kirchen, Regierungen und Intellektuellen kritisiert; und das, obwohl diesen Organisationen angehörige Leute selbst oft den Rat der Wahrsager suchen. Während der japanischen Besatzungszeit haben taiwanische Intellektuelle wie etwa Lijun Zhang , Xiantang Lin und Xinrong Wu zwar unterschiedliche Ansichten vertreten, doch war das Wahrsagen dennoch ein integraler Bestandteil ihres Lebens und das der Menschen aller Gesellschaftsschichten. Auch heute noch hat ein Großteil der Bevölkerung in Taiwan die Erfahrung etwa der Beschwichtigung der Gottheit ihres Geburtsjahres im traditionellen chinesischen 60-Jahres-Zyklus oder der Zukunftsvorhersage zur Auswahl ihres Namens. Hieran kann man erkennen, dass das Interesse der Menschen am Wahrsagen die Zeiten überdauert.

占卜的人們

Fortune-Telling and -Hearing

Die Menschen, welche wahrsagen

鐵口直斷

R.P.IOANNES ADAMVS SCHALL,GERMANVS
è Societate IESV. Pequini Supremi ac Regij Mathe.
matum Tribunalis Præses; indefeis 9 pro Conuersi.
one gentiu in Chinis Operarig ab auis 50.ætat:suæ 77.

G.A.Wolfgang.f:

湯若望
Johann Adam Schall von Bell

德籍耶穌會傳教士湯若望（Johann Adam Schall von Bell，1591-1666），於明末來到中國傳教，
擔任清代欽天監監正，引介了西洋天文曆算方法，重編《西洋曆法新書》，成為清代官方年曆《時
憲書》頒行，是見證曆占在東西文化交流的代表人物之一。

日耳曼國家博物館 藏／Paul Wolfgang Merkel'schen Familienstiftung 提供
Germanisches Nationalmuseum, Nuremberg, Germany. Lent by the Paul Wolfgang Merkel'schen Familienstiftung.

克卜勒魯道夫星曆表

Frontispiece Tabvlae Rudolphinae by Johannes Kepler

德國著名的數學家、天文學家約翰尼斯 · 克卜勒（Johannes Kepler），
是現代天文學的奠基者，相信哥白尼日心宇宙系統之說，也擅長占星術，常
幫人編算「出生圖」，賺取外快，但他不認為星座運勢就此決定了人的命運。
本件的「魯道夫星曆表」插圖，中心描繪當時主要天文辯論的代表人物—地
心說第谷（Tycho Brahe）與日心說哥白尼（Nicholas Copernicus）。

日耳曼國家博物館 藏
Germanisches Nationalmuseum, Nuremberg, Germany

紙牌算命
The Fortune Teller

18 世紀後期，紙牌算命開始在歐洲相當流行。本件描繪一位吉普賽裝扮的女性占卜師幫男士們解釋撲克牌的牌義，預測未來。

日耳曼國家博物館 藏
Germanisches Nationalmuseum,
Nuremberg, Germany

紙牌算命
The Card Layer

18 世紀後期，紙牌算命開始在歐洲相當流行。這幅諷刺漫畫「The Card Layer」，描繪了一位年老的女占卜師幫仕女們以撲克牌預測未來。

日耳曼國家博物館 藏
Germanisches Nationalmuseum, Nuremberg, Germany

占卜師瓷偶
The Fortune Teller

這二組 1770 年由德國著名瓷器廠路德維希堡（Ludwigsburg）生產的人物瓷偶，一組是站在噴泉旁的男性占星師幫年輕女子低聲解說，另一組是站在三腳桌前的女性手相師一手幫男士看手相、一手伸入他的口袋，呈現出歐洲啟蒙運動人們視占卜為騙術的態度。

日耳曼國家博物館 藏
Germanisches Nationalmuseum, Nuremberg, Germany

達邦社原住民治病祈禱明信片
A Postcard Showing an Indigenous
Tapangu Shaman Performing
Healing Ritual

鄒族達邦社巫師治病時，會手持沾有清水的楮
葉，灑在病人身上去病祈福。

國立臺灣歷史博物館 藏
2002.007.0825

陳俊傑繪《先生媽驅邪》
A Misshishi Performing Exorcism

描繪一名邵族「先生媽」（即女祭司）手持枝葉，正在為一名女子進行驅邪儀式。

國立臺灣歷史博物館 藏
2005.005.0059

不可思議的預言者來了廣告單
Flyer, "The Incredible Prophet Has Arrived."

日本時代有不少日本知名的命相師來臺，引進日本相學知識，多以骨相與手相為主。
本件即為宣傳東京下谷高島易斷研究部部長龍乘子約於大正 8（1919）年來臺看相
的廣告單，鑑定地點為臺中新盛橋通（今臺中車站前中山路一帶）的樋口旅館。

國立臺灣歷史博物館 藏
2018.024.0076

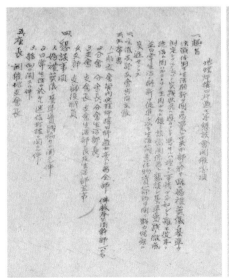

皇民奉公會溪湖分會地理師、
擇日師、道士等懇談會通知書
Note of Meeting for
Geomancers,
Day-selectors, and Taoist
Masters from the Xihu
Branch of Public Service
Association of Imperial
Subjects

皇民化時期皇民奉公會溪湖分會
於昭和 18（1943）年 5 月召開
會議，邀請溪湖地區的地理師、
擇日師、道士、賣卜者、佛教奉
公團等人員，一起討論如何協力
實踐婚禮與奠儀基準，及破除日
常生活的迷信等。

國立臺灣歷史博物館 藏
2019.011.0627.0003、2019.011.0627.0004

啟明堂嫁娶吉課堂徽印版
The Printing Forme of Qimingtang's Wedding Day Selection Sheet

啟明堂擇日館，為府城算命巷的百年老店，提供傳統八字算命、擇日、命名等服務。依刻印地址為臺南市中區，推測為 1945 年以後製作。

啟明堂擇日館　提供

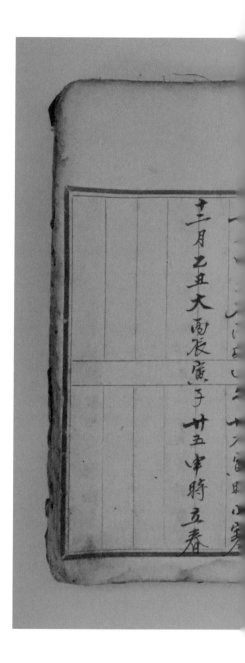

啟明堂擇日命卜印版
The Printing Forme of Qimingtang's Day Selection and Divination

啟明堂擇日館　提供

龜卦組
Turtle-shell Divination Set

啟明堂第三代傳人陳林曛，受日本教育長大，跟著父親陳樹根學習術數，20 歲開始接手家業，後傳子陳林泓。本件為其替人卜卦使用的龜卦組。

啟明堂擇日館　提供

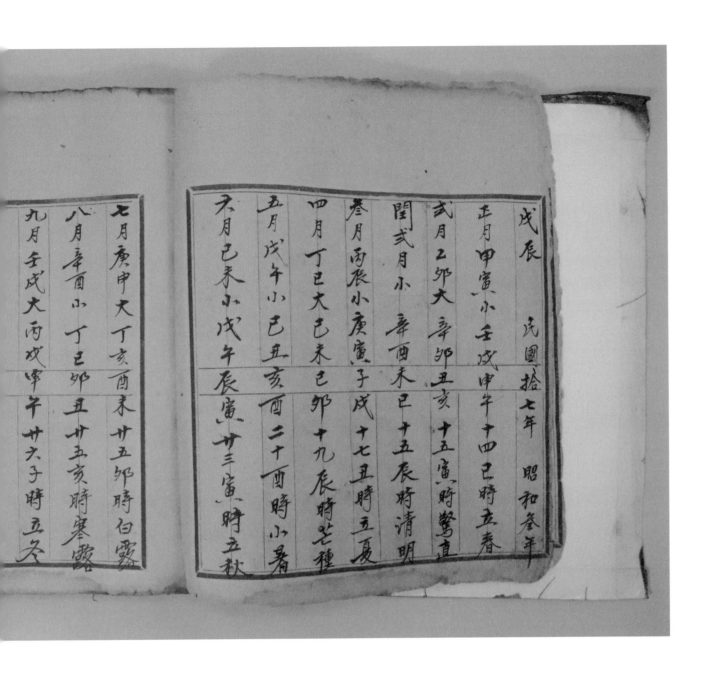

戊辰　民國拾七年　昭和叁年

正月甲寅小　壬戌申午十四巳時立春

式月乙卯大　辛卯丑亥十五寅時驚蟄

閏式月小　辛酉未巳十五辰將清明

叁月丙辰小　庚寅子戌十七丑時立夏

四月丁巳大　巳未卯十九辰時芒種

五月戊午小　巳丑亥二十酉時小暑

六月巳未小　戊午辰寅廿三寅時立秋

七月庚申大　丁亥酉未廿五卯時白露

八月辛酉小　丁巳卯丑廿五亥時寒露

九月壬戌大　丙戌申午廿六子時立冬

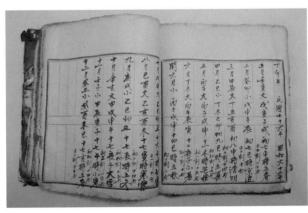

手抄節氣日誌
A Manuscript of Notes on Solar Terms

第三代陳林曛與第四代陳林泓父子傳承
手抄之擇日節氣日誌，記錄時間從昭和 2
（1927）年至民國 98（2009）年。

啟明堂擇日館 提供

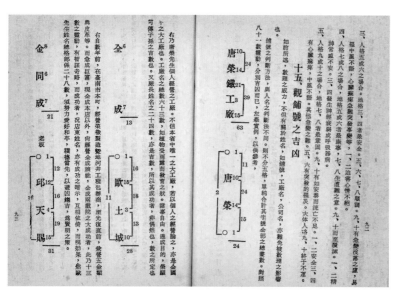

白惠文編著《姓名之命運學》
The Destiny in the Name

本書為「白惠文姓名學」創辦人白惠文增補《熊崎式姓名學之神秘》
之作,第1版於1950年出版,本件為1959年出版的第5版。

白惠文孫 提供

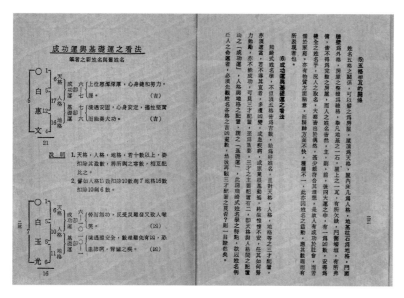

白惠文編著《姓名學之奧秘》
The Arcane of Onomancy

本書是白惠文第3本以姓名學為名的著作,於1959年出版。此頁面
是白惠文以自己改名為例,解釋成功運與基礎運。

白惠文孫 提供

白惠文與臺南市中區合作社人員合影
A Photo of Hui-wen Bai and Staff from the Tainan Central District Cooperative

熟悉合作法的白惠文，於戰後參與臺南市中區合作社（今臺南市第三信用合作社）的創設。圖為 1950 年 1 月白惠文（第 1 排右 2）與合作社人員合影，第 1 排左 2 推測可能為創社社長王鵬程。

白惠文孫 提供

熊崎健翁
Kumasaki Kenou

白惠文於 1933 年赴日與熊崎氏姓名學的創始者熊崎健翁（1882-1961）學習命理學，並將其著作《姓名の神秘》翻譯為漢文《熊崎式姓名學之神秘》。本圖為熊崎 77 歲所攝，寄贈予白氏留念。

白惠文孫 提供

白惠文替顧客看手相
Hui-wen Bai Reading Palms for a Customer

白惠文除以姓名學著名外，亦懂得易斷、測命、手相、面相等綜合命理學。

白惠文孫 提供

白惠文與邵禹銘合影
A Photo of Hui-wen Bai and Yu-ming Shao

白惠文原名白玉光（1887-1972），與產業組合的好友邵明，一起拜入日本東京五聖閣熊崎健翁門下。後來二人皆改名，邵氏改為禹銘，本圖為白惠文（左）與邵禹銘（右）當時學成的合影。

白惠文孫 提供

《一胎三個》電影劇照
The Triplet Film Still

1968 年上映，原名「抽籤卜卦」，由陳揚導演，石軍、張清清、矮仔財主演，是部描寫生育的笑料臺語片。

國立臺灣歷史博物館 藏
2003.009.0081

太王唱片出品《臺灣鄉土民謠全集：許石編曲指揮（4）》
Folksongs of Taiwan (4)

臺灣南部民謠〈卜卦調〉，呈現民間抽籤算命的詼諧、逗趣，被許石收納在其編曲的《臺灣鄉土民謠全集：許石編曲指揮》唱片。

國立臺灣歷史博物館 藏
2003.009.0669

捷發漢書部發行

看命問卜相褒全集

朋友大家那有榮　聽念相褒心恰滿　鳳山王个用心性　句豆做了上界明

只歌來听上界好　笑科問卜塊相褒　武號也是賢德做　買來恁通念廻廻

問卜相褒來廣起　甲恁諸君說透機　加治塊唱無意味　二人對答正有奇

我塊做人上打拼　為着腹肚出來行　那有影卦出牌區　卜看命

牌區寫甲全字句　另外三字命卜師　那有人卜問省事　即來參考袂恰須

想我做人即干苦　生理了卜講萬圓　有人看命折字數　想卜來問我前途

看命着我上界準　朗無用嘴甲人君　八字汝那廣　我着照命來斷分

看命問卜相褒歌

一

□發漢書部發行

汝那卜問我八字　二十五歲說透機　十月十九來出世　問卜好日暗見酉時

廿五門好鼠个相　只嗎照命來思量　我看甲人無親像　無相青暝先點香

真知汝都有影賢　看命朗無甲人包　要緊命底看甲透　看我東時能出頭

壬子年科辛亥月　丁未日牌有加襄　那無木象煞來生火　已酉被尅加連迴

汝廣日神有加熄　全望先生說照實　那無木象煞免的　出頭不知都一日

日神有影門丁未　有影元神有恰虛　十月火神加無氣　實在着廣照實正應該

十月个火盡樣呆　一个原由對都來　先生汝都說實在　着廣實在有影火加微

照看八字無通水　秋天火神小光輝　少年只斬難得貴　親像大雨遇亂雷

八字能來相鼠年　出世泰能門秋天　敢是閻王算錯見　只嗎正能安哖生

汝廣安哖是有影　一半也是八字命　果再尌酌詳細聽　好呆也是天註定

看命問卜相褒歌
A Duet Banter Song of Divination

王德賢於昭和11（1936）年撰寫以算命為主題的歌仔冊，以若干例子說明，先說一人生肖與年齡，講述此人的命運，有什麼樣的貴人，適合做哪種職業，又其婚姻應該配哪些對象，或者命中有否重大劫數等等，偶爾也間雜一些勸人為善的句子。

國立臺灣大學圖書館　藏

鶴標唱片發行〈問卜（上）〉
Fortunetelling (I)

鶴標唱片發行〈問卜（下）〉
Fortunetelling (II)

汪思明（1897-1969）是日本時代歌仔戲唱片的奠基者，擅於唸歌，本唱片即為汪思明以唸歌形式說唱算命師招呼客人來算命問卜的詼諧對話。

國立臺灣歷史博物館　藏

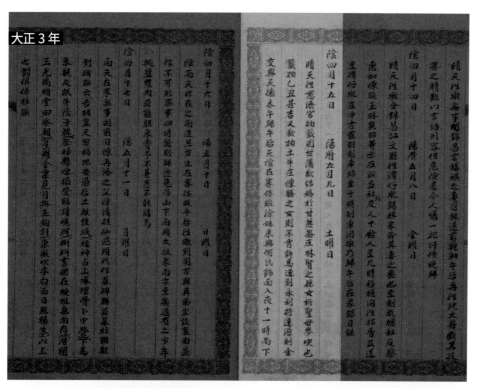

大正 3 年

昭和 3 年

張麗俊水竹居主人日記
The Diary of Li-jun Chang

臺中豐原士紳張麗俊（1868-1941），受過完整的傳統漢學教育，曾任保正、豐原街協議會員，積極參與廟宇、詩社等公共事務，對於兒女婚姻對象、疾病治療、家族墓地、遠行、家人未來運勢等生活課題時，通常會以求籤、找人卜卦與算命等占卜的方式決定。

中央研究院臺灣史研究所 提供

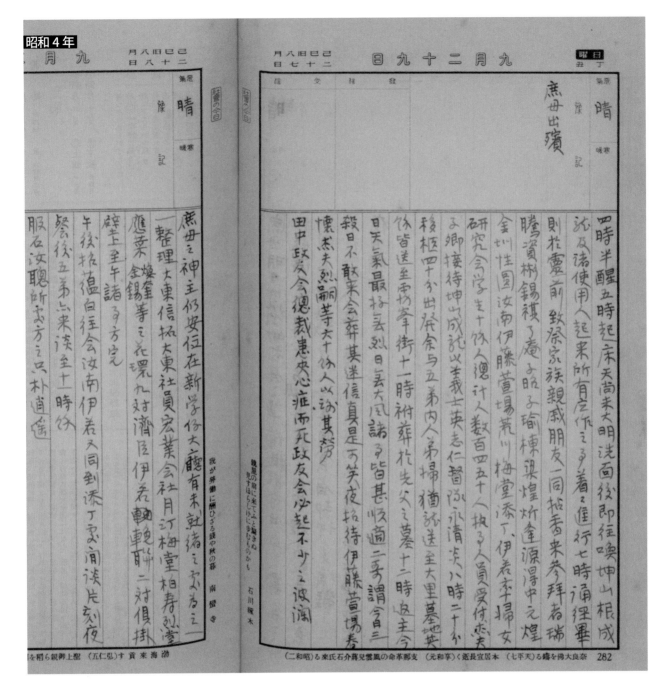

林獻堂灌園先生日記
The Diary of Hsien-tang Lin

受過傳統漢學教育，並常常接觸過西方知識的林獻堂（1881-1956），是臺中霧峰林家後代，曾任霧峰參事、區長，並於新民會、臺灣文化協會、臺灣民眾黨等組織擔任重要成員，認為扶乩、擇日沖煞等民間習俗為迷信陋習，主張打破迷信、改善社會習俗。

中央研究院臺灣史研究所 提供

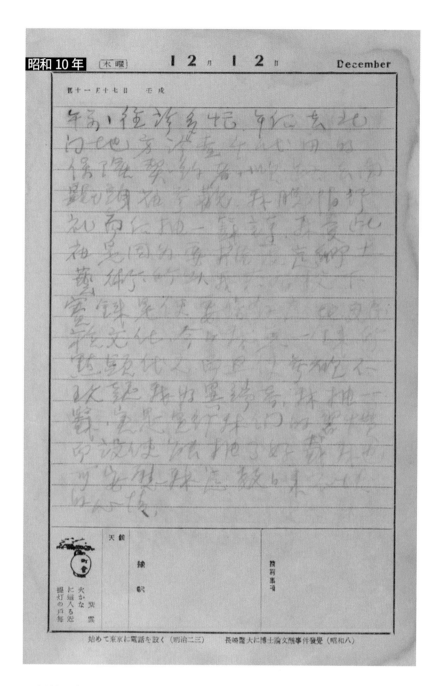

吳新榮日記
The Diary of Hsin-jung Wu

留學日本東京醫事專門學校的吳新榮（1907-1967），是位臺南的名醫，也是《民俗臺灣》編輯，積極推動臺灣文化的保存。作為受現代化教育的知識分子，他對於民間習俗自然是贊同改善迷信陋習，但同時他也因家人的習慣而默從，會去抽籤、求神問卜，也肯定占卜給人安慰的心理效果，非全然以科學理性思惟看待，進而重新省思傳統文化。

吳新榮家屬 提供／財團法人吳三連台灣史料基金會 藏

1935 年 12 月 12 日

原文文字：
午前，往診多忙。午后，去北門地方診查千代田的保險契約者，順路去南鯤鯓廟參觀。我脫帽行禮而后抽一籤詩，我愛此廟是因為要擁護這鄉土藝術，所以我若有投下賽錢，是使要保存這民族文化。今日我無一錢，以點頭代之，而且使參觀（者）不致疑我為異端者。我抽一籤，實是實行我們的習慣；而設使能抽了好籤，我也可安慰我這數日來不快的心情。

中央研究院臺灣史研究所 提供

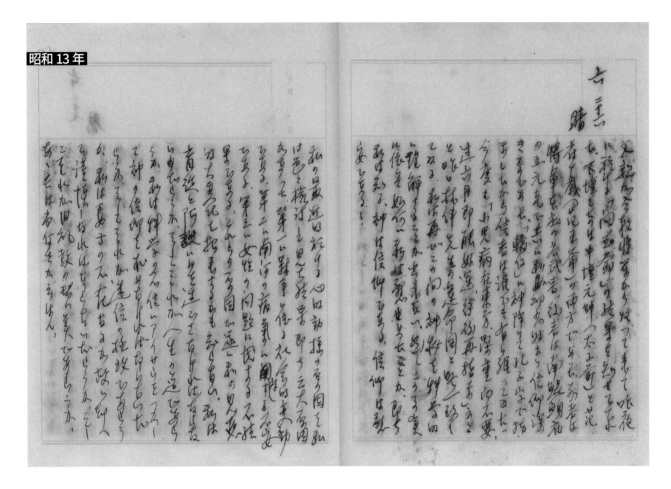

1938 年 6 月 26 日

原文文字：

父親今早由將軍回來，告訴我昨天「問王爺」的結果。降壇的是中壇元帥（太子爺）和范府千歲（范王爺）兩位，前者是將軍本庄的年輕武將，後者是南鯤鯓廟的五元老，兩尊都是我小時候就深切信仰的神明，降神在「轎仔」上，以孔子字指示信徒，每一信徒皆大為感恩。這次的指示是「小兒病在東方、沉重而不要過六月即能好運，待後再指示」。和昨日林泮先生所指示的運命圖是一致的。我仍然不能以科學性來理解這中間的神秘感。然而由此事實，我知道我所得到的安慰是對神明的一種信仰。信仰就是安慰。

我對自己最近在精神上的動搖原因，做了一番檢討。結果有三個原因：第一、因戰爭所致的社會之變動。第二、因南河的病導致的不安。第三、有關女性問題的未解決。可能這些原因招來我思想的大變化。我該以盲從和阿諛的方式過日子嗎？或者這是人生之道嗎？或不相信科學，唾棄科學而做求神問卜的信仰呢？這是迷信的極致嗎？是否因妻子不在，我反而更要謹慎些才行呢？這些是對舊禮教的讚美嗎？啊！我還能說甚麼呢？

中央研究院臺灣史研究所 提供

06

占卜與遊戲

Divinations and Games
Wahrsagung und Spiel

以占卜預測未來，往往和風險評估相關，也因之與骰子、紙牌等博弈遊戲，講求機率相類，帶有遊戲、娛樂、社交的和解答命運的性質。最典型的即是 19 世紀盛行的塔羅牌，透過牌卡解答短時間的問題，並解析自我的潛意識。臺灣則有鳥卦籤牌，趣味性與塔羅牌相仿。

隨著科技的發達，占卜工具走向線上化、遊戲化，解讀不再是占卜者專有的權力，預測結果成為凸顯個人特質與自我表述的一種方式。占卜除了心理療癒的效果，也成為社交聯誼的媒介。在現代步調極快、生活緊張的社會形態，不失為一種認識自我、人與自然、人際關係和追求和諧的輕鬆方法。

今天，你想問命運什麼問題？你怎麼看待占卜給你的答案？

✖

Predicting the future with divination always involves risk assessment. In addition to wagering on probabilities, divination can take the form of a game of chance, such as dice or cards, featuring gaming, entertainment, and socializing, while providing insight into one's destiny. One classic example is tarot cards. Players use tarot cards, popularized in Europe during the 19th century, to answer questions and analyze their subconscious. Taiwan has "bird divination" which is similar to tarot cards, but a bird draws cards to answer questions.

As technology has developed, tools for divination have become digitalized and gamified, so that fortune-tellers no longer "corner" the fortune-telling market. Predictions have become a way to highlight personal characteristics and self-expression. Not only does divination provide a certain degree of psychological healing, but also serves as a way to socialize. Living in a fast-paced and uptight modern world, divination can also be considered a casual approach to understanding self and to balancing the relationship between the individual, nature, and society.

What questions do you have today about your destiny?
What do you think of the answers given to you through fortune telling?

Die Vorhersage der Zukunft durch Wahrsagen wird oft mit einer Risikoeinschätzung in Verbindung gebracht und ähnelt daher Wettspielen wie Würfel- oder Kartenspiel. Es legt großen Stellenwert auf Wahrscheinlichkeit und trägt den Charakter von Spiel, Unterhaltung, sozialem Austausch und der Beantwortung des Schicksals. Das klassischste Beispiel hierfür ist das im 19. Jahrhundert florierende Tarot, bei dem mittels Karten in kurzer Zeit Fragen beantwortet werden und man sein Unterbewusstsein analysieren kann. In Taiwan hingegen gibt es das Spiel der Vogel-Trigramme, bei dem ein Vogel Orakelplättchen zieht und dessen Interessantheit der des Tarot ähnelt.

Im Zuge des technischen Fortschritts sind die Werkzeuge des Wahrsagens zunehmend online verfügbar und immer stärker spielhaft interpretiert, sodass die Interprätation nicht länger das alleinige Privileg des Wahrsagers ist. Das Resultat einer Voraussage wird zu einem Mittel, um persönliche Eigenschaften hervorzuheben und sich selbst auszudrücken. Außer der psychischen Behandlung wird das Wahrsagen außerdem ein Medium des sozialen Kontakts und der Freundschaft. In unserer modernen Gesellschaftsform mit ihrem schnellen Tempo und stressvollen Leben kann es nach wie vor als eine entspannte Methode gelten, sich selbst, Mensch und Natur, und zwischenpersönliche Beziehungen kennen zu lernen und Harmonie anzustreben.

Welche Frage möchtest du dem Schicksal heute stellen?
Was hältst du von der Antwort, die das Wahrsagen dir gibt?

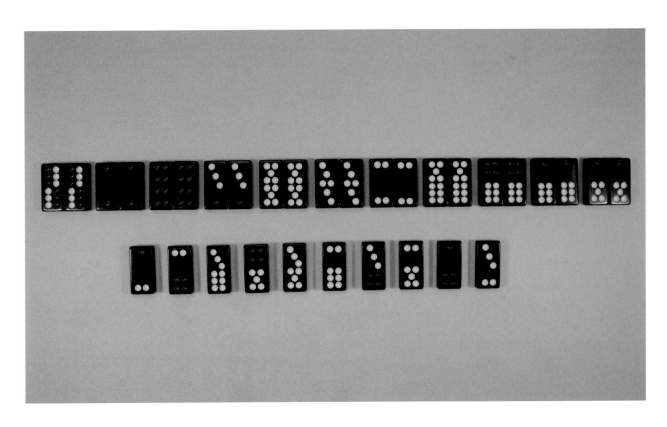

中國骨牌
Chinese Dominos

中國骨牌，又稱牙牌，計有 32 隻牌，原是賭博遊戲的用具，清代發展出《牙牌神數》的占卜方式，方法為「全副牙牌一字排，中間看有幾多開，連排三次分明記，上下中平內取裁。」即將全副牙牌洗成一排，以牌組的開數對照籤文，判讀吉凶。

骰子組
Dice Set

擲骰子，是古老的賭博遊戲，也曾用於占卜，透過隨機投擲的方式進行占卜。

國立臺灣歷史博物館 藏
2005.010.0244

天地牌中國撲克牌
Tiandi Chinese Porkers Cards

1970-1980 年代使用的天地牌中國撲克牌，計 60 張牌，是由中國的天干、
地支及五行變化而成，花色主要由二類（天、地）、三色（紅、綠、黑）及
六花（日、月、星、梅、竹、松）組成。遊戲人數為 2-6 人，可玩撿點、接
龍、橋牌、吹牛、13 點等 9 種遊戲。除遊戲外，可將各花色的 3、4、5、6、
7 集合而成 30 張「五行牌」，用於卜卦及占卜。

國立臺灣歷史博物館 藏／蔡政芳捐贈
2015.035.0009

鳥卦籤牌組
Bird Divination Lottery Set

鳥卦，又稱鳥仔卦，是臺灣時下年輕人流行、具遊戲性的占卜方法。操作上先以白紋鳥叼出籤牌，命理師再針對抽出的籤牌圖案進行解說。鳥卦籤牌有 24、36、60 張等之分，以 24 張的文王卦 24 籤為常見，繪有傳統歷史故事。本組手繪籤牌計 24 張，每張皆有籤題，無籤詩正文。

國立臺灣歷史博物館 藏
2018.024.0077、2018.024.0078、2018.024.0079、2018.024.0080

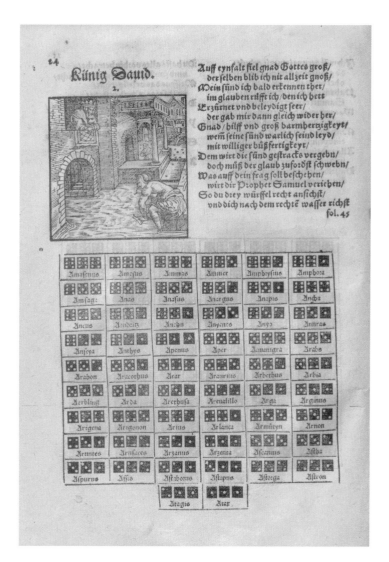

《紀念瑪麗亞皇后的算命書》
The *Lot Book in Honour of the Roman, Hungarian, and Bohemian Queen*

基督教教義將藉由抽籤諮詢神諭的做法視為異教、迷信，然而卻無法阻止這種做法的持續流行。同時中世紀後期民間有些書籍將其轉化為娛樂，宣稱這是有趣的遊戲而非占卜。本書於1546年出版，用以紀念神聖羅馬帝國、匈牙利、和波西米亞皇后瑪麗亞（Maria of Austria），書中利用擲骰子及一套參考聖經的複雜系統，讓讀者取得答案的同時，也獲得娛樂與啟發。

日耳曼國家博物館 藏
Germanisches Nationalmuseum, Nuremberg, Germany

《算命的水星》
The *Fortune-Telling Mercurius*

本書於1717年在德國紐倫堡出版，針對男性、女性讀者提供100多個問題解答，作為人們聚會消遣娛樂之用。

日耳曼國家博物館 藏
Germanisches Nationalmuseum, Nuremberg, Germany

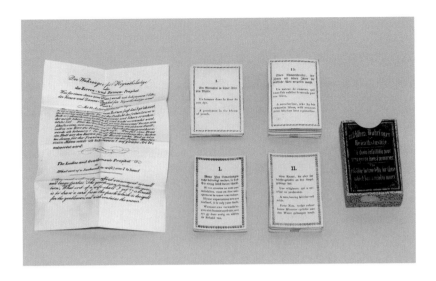

結婚算命卡

Infallible Fortune-Teller for Those Eager to Marry

這副紙牌於 1830-1850 年發行，計有 64 張，依男女性別分為黃、白二種紙牌顏色，解答了「我未來的妻子或丈夫將是什麼樣的人？」的答案。紙牌上印有德文、法文、英文等 3 種語言，可流通於德文、英文、法文市場。

日耳曼國家博物館 藏
Germanisches Nationalmuseum, Nuremberg, Germany

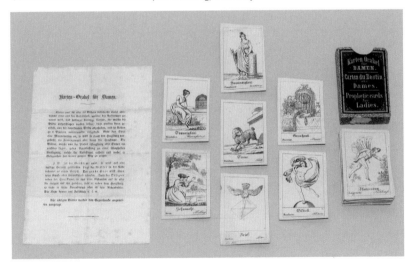

女士預言卡

Prophetic Cards for Ladies

約於 1830 年發行的算命紙牌，計有 30 張牌，印有德文、法文、英文 3 種語言印刷。雖名為「女士預言卡」，提供給中產階級男女玩家使用。玩牌的方式是由一個人當莊家，決定發牌給誰，再用玩家的智慧解讀牌義。例如收到牧師圖卡的人代表會很快結婚。

日耳曼國家博物館 藏
Germanisches Nationalmuseum, Nuremberg, Germany

雷諾曼卡
Lenormand Fortune-Telling Cards

本件為早期的版本，印製於 1800-1850 年間，計有 36 張。雷諾曼卡與法國占卜師瑪
麗 · 安妮 · 雷諾曼（Marie Anne Lenormand）同名，於 18 世紀由德國商人約
翰 · 卡斯帕 · 赫克特爾（Johann Kaspar Hechtel）設計，最初作為一種牌卡遊戲，
並非用於占卜目的。牌卡圖案元素來自日常生活中常見的人事物，例如：男人、女人、
小孩、錨、騎士、房屋、太陽等。

日耳曼國家博物館 藏
Germanisches Nationalmuseum, Nuremberg, Germany

德文版大埃特利亞塔羅牌
Grand Etteilla I

將塔羅牌從遊戲轉變為占卜用途的關鍵人物是法國神秘學家尚巴普蒂斯特瓦 · 阿雷特（Jean-Baptiste Alliette），他設計了更適合占卜的大埃特利亞塔羅牌（Grand Etteilla），Etteilla 是 Alliette 姓名倒寫的化名。本件 1793 年的德文版大埃特利亞塔羅牌，相當稀少，是大埃特利亞塔羅牌的圖案與名稱轉換為德文的最佳見證。

日耳曼國家博物館 藏
Germanisches Nationalmuseum, Nuremberg, Germany

塔羅精靈
The Tarot Elves

知名漫畫家游素蘭繪製，於1998年發
行之塔羅牌，計有22張大牌，標榜
「游素蘭的愛情遊方箋」，「首創漫
畫圖解教學」，是臺灣設計塔羅牌的
發展形式之一。

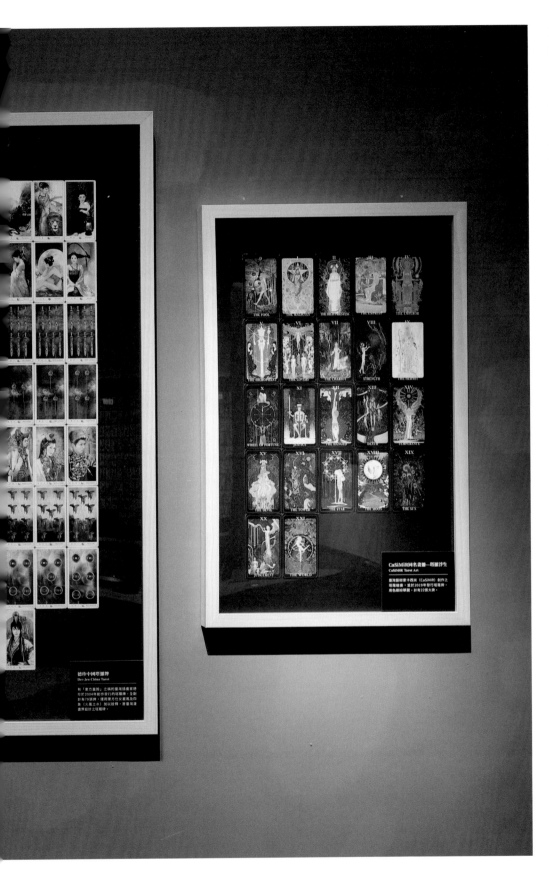

德珍中國塔羅牌
Der-Jen China Tarot

有「東方畫姬」之稱的臺灣插畫家德珍於2004年創作發行的塔羅牌，全副計有78張牌，運用東方仕女畫風及四象（火風土水）加以詮釋，是臺灣漫畫界設計之塔羅牌。

CaSiMiR同名畫冊─塔羅浮生
CaSiMiR Tarot Art

臺灣藝術家卡西米（CaSiMiR）創作之塔羅繪畫，並於2019年發行塔羅牌，用色繽紛華麗，計有22張大牌。

左｜塔羅精靈
Left｜The Tarot Elves

知名漫畫家游素蘭繪製、於1998年發行之塔羅牌，計有22張大牌，標榜「游素蘭的愛情處方箋」、「首創漫畫圖解教學」，是臺灣設計塔羅牌的發展形式之一。

中｜德珍中國塔羅牌
Middle｜Der-Jen China Tarot

有「東方畫姬」之稱的臺灣插畫家德珍於2004年創作發行的塔羅牌，全副計有78張牌，運用東方仕女畫風及四象（火風土水）加以詮釋，是臺灣漫畫界設計之塔羅牌。

右｜CaSiMiR同名畫冊─塔羅浮生
Right｜CaSiMiR Tarot Art

臺灣藝術家卡西米（CaSiMiR）創作之塔羅繪畫，並於2019年發行塔羅牌，用色繽紛華麗，計有22張大牌。

感 謝 Acknowledgements

以下單位及個人提供文物、圖像影音授權、資訊及諮詢協助充實本展覽
（依姓氏筆畫及字母排列）

個人

丁淑嬌
于禮本
王思迅
白宗民
朱彥銘
孟小靖
林柏樑
祝平一
施雨辰
洪振齊
張詠詠
陳冠彰
黃朱平
魏丹
謝宗榮
Christopher J. Findler
Achim Kehlenbach
Michael Lackner
Ulrike Ludwig

單位

民間全民電視股份有限公司
南天書局有限公司
財團法人吳三連臺灣史料基金會
財團法人原住民族文化事業基金會
國立臺灣大學圖書館
國立臺灣博物館
啟明堂擇日館
國家圖書館
漢珍數位圖書股份有限公司

德國「此命當何特展」團隊

林玉雲
蔡芷芳
Thomas Eser
Marie-Therese Feist
Michael Lackner
Ulrike Ludwig
Heike Zech

策展團隊

指導單位

主辦單位

合辦單位

展覽策辦

研究策展｜張淑卿
展示策展｜周宜穎
單元文字審訂｜祝平一

統籌指導｜張隆志
行政指導｜楊仙妃、李雪敬
展覽統籌｜江明珊
展覽專案管理及執行｜周宜穎、余孟璇、江瑄
典藏規劃執行｜陳靜寬、黃瀞慧、鄭勤思
行銷推廣｜吳佳霓、吳孟青、吳如媚
展覽導覽｜蕭軒竹、黃俞嘉
展場協力與維護管理｜周哲宇、陳明祥
展場設計製作｜起子創意設計股份有限公司
文物佈展｜鄭勤思、禾勤藝術有限公司
文物數位化作業｜杜偉誌、呂錦瀚、耀點設計有限公司

本展覽為文化部 110 年度「行銷國家品牌進入國際」之一

國家圖書館出版品預行編目 (CIP) 資料

算×命：歐洲與臺灣的占卜特展展覽專刊＝Calculating×
Destiny : Divinatoin in Europe and Taiwan／朗宓樹，烏爾
里克路德維希，祝平一，張淑卿專文撰寫；江明珊總編輯 . --
初版 . -- 臺南市：國立臺灣歷史博物館，2022.04
　　面；　公分
ISBN 978-986-532-577-0（平裝）
1.CST: 占卜　2.CST: 文物展示　3.CST: 博物館展覽

292　　　　　　　　　　　　　　111005281

算 × 命：歐洲與臺灣的占卜特展展覽專刊
Calculating × Destiny:
Divination in Europe and Taiwan

發行人｜張隆志

專文撰寫｜朗宓榭、烏爾里克路德維希、祝平一、張淑卿（依文章順序）

總編輯｜江明珊

執行編輯｜周宜穎、張淑卿

翻譯｜汪怡君、Christoph Henninger

美術設計｜起子創意設計股份有限公司

印刷｜奇異多媒體印藝有限公司

出版發行｜國立臺灣歷史博物館

　　　　　臺南市安南區長和路一段 250 號

　　　　　電話｜06-3568889

　　　　　傳真｜06-3564981

　　　　　http://www.nmth.gov.tw/

定價｜新臺幣 360 元

出版日期｜2022 年 4 月初版

GPN｜1011100489

ISBN｜978-986-532-577-0